AGAINST APION

Start Publishing PD LLC
Copyright © 2024 by Start Publishing PD LLC

All rights reserved, including the right to reproduce this book or portions thereof in any form whatsoever.

Start Publishing PD is a registered trademark of Start Publishing PD LLC
Manufactured in the United States of America

Cover art: Shutterstock/Taisiya Kozorez

Cover design: Jennifer Do

10 9 8 7 6 5 4 3 2 1

ISBN 979-8-8809-0132-6

AGAINST APION[1]
by Flavius Josephus
Translated by William Whiston

BOOK I

1. I Suppose that by my books of the Antiquity of the Jews, most excellent Epaphroditus, [2] have made it evident to those who peruse them, that our Jewish nation is of very great antiquity, and had a distinct subsistence of its own originally; as also, I have therein declared how we came to inhabit this country wherein we now live. Those Antiquities contain the history of five thousand years, and are taken out of our sacred books, but are translated by me into the Greek tongue. However, since I observe a considerable number of people giving ear to the reproaches that are laid against us by those who bear ill-will to us, and will not believe what I have written concerning the antiquity of our nation, while they take it for a plain sign that our nation is of a late date, because they are not so much as vouchsafed a bare mention by the most famous historiographers among the Grecians. I therefore have thought myself under an obligation to write somewhat briefly about these subjects, in order to convict those that reproach us of spite and voluntary falsehood, and to correct the ignorance of others, and withal to instruct all those who are desirous of knowing the truth of what great antiquity we really are. As for the witnesses whom I shall produce for the proof of what I say, they shall be such as are esteemed to be of the greatest reputation for truth, and the most skillful in the knowledge of all antiquity by the Greeks themselves. I will also show, that those who have written so reproachfully and falsely about us are to be convicted by what they have written themselves to the contrary. I shall also endeavor to give an account of the reasons why it hath so happened, that there have not been a great number of Greeks who have made mention of our nation in their histories. I will, however, bring those Grecians to light who have not omitted such our history, for the sake of those that either do not know them, or pretend not to know them already.

2. And now, in the first place, I cannot but greatly wonder at those men, who suppose that we must attend to none but Grecians, when we are inquiring about the most ancient facts, and must inform ourselves of their truth from them only, while we must not believe ourselves nor other men; for I am convinced that the very reverse is the truth of the case. I mean this,—if we will not be led by vain opinions, but will make inquiry after truth from facts themselves; for they will find that almost all which concerns the Greeks happened not long ago; nay, one may say, is of yesterday only. I speak of the building of their cities, the inventions of

their arts, and the description of their laws; and as for their care about the writing down of their histories, it is very near the last thing they set about. However, they acknowledge themselves so far, that they were the Egyptians, the Chaldeans, and the Phoenicians (for I will not now reckon ourselves among them) that have preserved the memorials of the most ancient and most lasting traditions of mankind; for almost all these nations inhabit such countries as are least subject to destruction from the world about them; and these also have taken especial care to have nothing omitted of what was [remarkably] done among them; but their history was esteemed sacred, and put into public tables, as written by men of the greatest wisdom they had among them. But as for the place where the Grecians inhabit, ten thousand destructions have overtaken it, and blotted out the memory of former actions; so that they were ever beginning a new way of living, and supposed that every one of them was the origin of their new state. It was also late, and with difficulty, that they came to know the letters they now use; for those who would advance their use of these letters to the greatest antiquity pretend that they learned them from the Phoenicians and from Cadmus; yet is nobody able to demonstrate that they have any writing preserved from that time, neither in their temples, nor in any other public monuments. This appears, because the time when those lived who went to the Trojan war, so many years afterward, is in great doubt, and great inquiry is made, whether the Greeks used their letters at that time; and the most prevailing opinion, and that nearest the truth, is, that their present way of using those letters was unknown at that time. However, there is not any writing which the Greeks agree to be genuine among them ancienter than Homer's Poems, who must plainly he confessed later than the siege of Troy; nay, the report goes, that even he did not leave his poems in writing, but that their memory was preserved in songs, and they were put together afterward, and that this is the reason of such a number of variations as are found in them. [3] As for those who set themselves about writing their histories, I mean such as Cadmus of Miletus, and Acusilaus of Argos, and any others that may be mentioned as succeeding Acusilaus, they lived but a little while before the Persian expedition into Greece. But then for those that first introduced philosophy, and the consideration of things celestial and divine among them, such as Pherceydes the Syrian, and Pythagoras, and Thales, all with one consent agree, that they learned what they knew of the Egyptians and Chaldeans, and wrote but little And these are the things which are supposed to be the oldest of all among the Greeks; and they have much ado to believe that the writings ascribed to those men are genuine.

3. How can it then be other than an absurd thing, for the Greeks to be so

proud, and to vaunt themselves to be the only people that are acquainted with antiquity, and that have delivered the true accounts of those early times after an accurate manner? Nay, who is there that cannot easily gather from the Greek writers themselves, that they knew but little on any good foundation when they set to write, but rather wrote their histories from their own conjectures? Accordingly, they confute one another in their own books to purpose, and are not ashamed. to give us the most contradictory accounts of the same things; and I should spend my time to little purpose, if I should pretend to teach the Greeks that which they know better than I already, what a great disagreement there is between Hellanicus and Acusilaus about their genealogies; in how many eases Acusilaus corrects Hesiod: or after what manner Ephorus demonstrates Hellanicus to have told lies in the greatest part of his history; as does Timeus in like manner as to Ephorus, and the succeeding writers do to Timeus, and all the later writers do to Herodotus nor could Timeus agree with Antiochus and Philistius, or with Callias, about the Sicilian History, no more than do the several writers of the Athide follow one another about the Athenian affairs; nor do the historians the like, that wrote the Argolics, about the affairs of the Argives. And now what need I say any more about particular cities and smaller places, while in the most approved writers of the expedition of the Persians, and of the actions which were therein performed, there are so great differences? Nay, Thucydides himself is accused of some as writing what is false, although he seems to have given us the exactest history of the affairs of his own time. [4]

4. As for the occasions of so great disagreement of theirs, there may be assigned many that are very probable, if any have a mind to make an inquiry about them; but I ascribe these contradictions chiefly to two causes, which I will now mention, and still think what I shall mention in the first place to be the principal of all. For if we remember that in the beginning the Greeks had taken no care to have public records of their several transactions preserved, this must for certain have afforded those that would afterward write about those ancient transactions the opportunity of making mistakes, and the power of making lies also; for this original recording of such ancient transactions hath not only been neglected by the other states of Greece, but even among the Athenians themselves also, who pretend to be Aborigines, and to have applied themselves to learning, there are no such records extant; nay, they say themselves that the laws of Draco concerning murders, which are now extant in writing, are the most ancient of their public records; which Draco yet lived but a little before the tyrant Pisistratus. [5] For as to the Arcadians, who make such boasts of their antiquity, what need I speak of them in particular, since it was still later before they got their letters, and learned them,

and that with difficulty also. [6]

5. There must therefore naturally arise great differences among writers, when they had no original records to lay for their foundation, which might at once inform those who had an inclination to learn, and contradict those that would tell lies. However, we are to suppose a second occasion besides the former of these contradictions; it is this: That those who were the most zealous to write history were not solicitous for the discovery of truth, although it was very easy for them always to make such a profession; but their business was to demonstrate that they could write well, and make an impression upon mankind thereby; and in what manner of writing they thought they were able to exceed others, to that did they apply themselves, Some of them betook themselves to the writing of fabulous narrations; some of them endeavored to please the cities or the kings, by writing in their commendation; others of them fell to finding faults with transactions, or with the writers of such transactions, and thought to make a great figure by so doing. And indeed these do what is of all things the most contrary to true history; for it is the great character of true history that all concerned therein both speak and write the same things; while these men, by writing differently about the same things, think they shall be believed to write with the greatest regard to truth. We therefore [who are Jews] must yield to the Grecian writers as to language and eloquence of composition; but then we shall give them no such preference as to the verity of ancient history, and least of all as to that part which concerns the affairs of our own several countries.

6. As to the care of writing down the records from the earliest antiquity among the Egyptians and Babylonians; that the priests were intrusted therewith, and employed a philosophical concern about it; that they were the Chaldean priests that did so among the Babylonians; and that the Phoenicians, who were mingled among the Greeks, did especially make use of their letters, both for the common affairs of life, and for the delivering down the history of common transactions, I think I may omit any proof, because all men allow it so to be. But now as to our forefathers, that they took no less care about writing such records, [for I will not say they took greater care than the others I spoke of,] and that they committed that matter to their high priests and to their prophets, and that these records have been written all along down to our own times with the utmost accuracy; nay, if it be not too bold for me to say it, our history will be so written hereafter;—I shall endeavor briefly to inform you.

7. For our forefathers did not only appoint the best of these priests, and those that attended upon the Divine worship, for that design from the beginning, but made provision that the stock of the priests should continue unmixed and pure;

for he who is partaker of the priesthood must propagate of a wife of the same nation, without having any regard to money, or any other dignities; but he is to make a scrutiny, and take his wife's genealogy from the ancient tables, and procure many witnesses to it.[7] And this is our practice not only in Judea, but wheresoever any body of men of our nation do live; and even there an exact catalogue of our priests' marriages is kept; I mean at Egypt and at Babylon, or in any other place of the rest of the habitable earth, whithersoever our priests are scattered; for they send to Jerusalem the ancient names of their parents in writing, as well as those of their remoter ancestors, and signify who are the witnesses also. But if any war falls out, such as have fallen out a great many of them already, when Antiochus Epiphanes made an invasion upon our country, as also when Pompey the Great and Quintilius Varus did so also, and principally in the wars that have happened in our own times, those priests that survive them compose new tables of genealogy out of the old records, and examine the circumstances of the women that remain; for still they do not admit of those that have been captives, as suspecting that they had conversation with some foreigners. But what is the strongest argument of our exact management in this matter is what I am now going to say, that we have the names of our high priests from father to son set down in our records for the interval of two thousand years; and if any of these have been transgressors of these rules, they are prohibited to present themselves at the altar, or to be partakers of any other of our purifications; and this is justly, or rather necessarily done, because every one is not permitted of his own accord to be a writer, nor is there any disagreement in what is written; they being only prophets that have written the original and earliest accounts of things as they learned them of God himself by inspiration; and others have written what hath happened in their own times, and that in a very distinct manner also.

8. For we have not an innumerable multitude of books among us, disagreeing from and contradicting one another, [as the Greeks have,] but only twenty-two books,[8] which contain the records of all the past times; which are justly believed to be divine; and of them five belong to Moses, which contain his laws and the traditions of the origin of mankind till his death. This interval of time was little short of three thousand years; but as to the time from the death of Moses till the reign of Artaxerxes king of Persia, who reigned after Xerxes, the prophets, who were after Moses, wrote down what was done in their times in thirteen books. The remaining four books contain hymns to God, and precepts for the conduct of human life. It is true, our history hath been written since Artaxerxes very particularly, but hath not been esteemed of the like authority with the former by our forefathers, because there hath not been an exact succession of prophets since

that time; and how firmly we have given credit to these books of our own nation is evident by what we do; for during so many ages as have already passed, no one has been so bold as either to add any thing to them, to take any thing from them, or to make any change in them; but it is become natural to all Jews immediately, and from their very birth, to esteem these books to contain Divine doctrines, and to persist in them, and, if occasion be willingly to die for them. For it is no new thing for our captives, many of them in number, and frequently in time, to be seen to endure racks and deaths of all kinds upon the theatres, that they may not be obliged to say one word against our laws and the records that contain them; whereas there are none at all among the Greeks who would undergo the least harm on that account, no, nor in case all the writings that are among them were to be destroyed; for they take them to be such discourses as are framed agreeably to the inclinations of those that write them; and they have justly the same opinion of the ancient writers, since they see some of the present generation bold enough to write about such affairs, wherein they were not present, nor had concern enough to inform themselves about them from those that knew them; examples of which may be had in this late war of ours, where some persons have written histories, and published them, without having been in the places concerned, or having been near them when the actions were done; but these men put a few things together by hearsay, and insolently abuse the world, and call these writings by the name of Histories.

9. As for myself, I have composed a true history of that whole war, and of all the particulars that occurred therein, as having been concerned in all its transactions; for I acted as general of those among us that are named Galileans, as long as it was possible for us to make any opposition. I was then seized on by the Romans, and became a captive. Vespasian also and Titus had me kept under a guard, and forced me to attend them continually. At the first I was put into bonds, but was set at liberty afterward, and sent to accompany Titus when he came from Alexandria to the siege of Jerusalem; during which time there was nothing done which escaped my knowledge; for what happened in the Roman camp I saw, and wrote down carefully; and what informations the deserters brought [out of the city], I was the only man that understood them. Afterward I got leisure at Rome; and when all my materials were prepared for that work, I made use of some persons to assist me in learning the Greek tongue, and by these means I composed the history of those transactions. And I was so well assured of the truth of what I related, that I first of all appealed to those that had the supreme command in that war, Vespasian and Titus, as witnesses for me, for to them I presented those books first of all, and after them to many of the Romans who had been in the war. I also

sold them to many of our own men who understood the Greek philosophy; among whom were Julius Archelaus, Herod [king of Chalcis], a person of great gravity, and king Agrippa himself, a person that deserved the greatest admiration. Now all these men bore their testimony to me, that I had the strictest regard to truth; who yet would not have dissembled the matter, nor been silent, if I, out of ignorance, or out of favor to any side, either had given false colors to actions, or omitted any of them.

10. There have been indeed some bad men, who have attempted to calumniate my history, and took it to be a kind of scholastic performance for the exercise of young men. A strange sort of accusation and calumny this! since every one that undertakes to deliver the history of actions truly ought to know them accurately himself in the first place, as either having been concerned in them himself, or been informed of them by such as knew them. Now both these methods of knowledge I may very properly pretend to in the composition of both my works; for, as I said, I have translated the Antiquities out of our sacred books; which I easily could do, since I was a priest by my birth, and have studied that philosophy which is contained in those writings: and for the History of the War, I wrote it as having been an actor myself in many of its transactions, an eye-witness in the greatest part of the rest, and was not unacquainted with any thing whatsoever that was either said or done in it. How impudent then must those deserve to be esteemed that undertake to contradict me about the true state of those affairs! who, although they pretend to have made use of both the emperors' own memoirs, yet could not they he acquainted with our affairs who fought against them.

11. This digression I have been obliged to make out of necessity, as being desirous to expose the vanity of those that profess to write histories; and I suppose I have sufficiently declared that this custom of transmitting down the histories of ancient times hath been better preserved by those nations which are called Barbarians, than by the Greeks themselves. I am now willing, in the next place, to say a few things to those that endeavor to prove that our constitution is but of late time, for this reason, as they pretend, that the Greek writers have said nothing about us; after which I shall produce testimonies for our antiquity out of the writings of foreigners; I shall also demonstrate that such as cast reproaches upon our nation do it very unjustly.

12. As for ourselves, therefore, we neither inhabit a maritime country, nor do we delight in merchandise, nor in such a mixture with other men as arises from it; but the cities we dwell in are remote from the sea, and having a fruitful country for our habitation, we take pains in cultivating that only. Our principal care of all

is this, to educate our children well; and we think it to be the most necessary business of our whole life to observe the laws that have been given us, and to keep those rules of piety that have been delivered down to us. Since, therefore, besides what we have already taken notice of, we have had a peculiar way of living of our own, there was no occasion offered us in ancient ages for intermixing among the Greeks, as they had for mixing among the Egyptians, by their intercourse of exporting and importing their several goods; as they also mixed with the Phoenicians, who lived by the sea-side, by means of their love of lucre in trade and merchandise. Nor did our forefathers betake themselves, as did some others, to robbery; nor did they, in order to gain more wealth, fall into foreign wars, although our country contained many ten thousands of men of courage sufficient for that purpose. For this reason it was that the Phoenicians themselves came soon by trading and navigation to be known to the Grecians, and by their means the Egyptians became known to the Grecians also, as did all those people whence the Phoenicians in long voyages over the seas carried wares to the Grecians. The Medes also and the Persians, when they were lords of Asia, became well known to them; and this was especially true of the Persians, who led their armies as far as the other continent [Europe]. The Thracians were also known to them by the nearness of their countries, and the Scythians by the means of those that sailed to Pontus; for it was so in general that all maritime nations, and those that inhabited near the eastern or western seas, became most known to those that were desirous to be writers; but such as had their habitations further from the sea were for the most part unknown to them which things appear to have happened as to Europe also, where the city of Rome, that hath this long time been possessed of so much power, and hath performed such great actions in war, is yet never mentioned by Herodotus, nor by Thucydides, nor by any one of their contemporaries; and it was very late, and with great difficulty, that the Romans became known to the Greeks. Nay, those that were reckoned the most exact historians [and Ephorus for one] were so very ignorant of the Gauls and the Spaniards, that he supposed the Spaniards, who inhabit so great a part of the western regions of the earth, to be no more than one city. Those historians also have ventured to describe such customs as were made use of by them, which they never had either done or said; and the reason why these writers did not know the truth of their affairs was this, that they had not any commerce together; but the reason why they wrote such falsities was this, that they had a mind to appear to know things which others had not known. How can it then be any wonder, if our nation was no more known to many of the Greeks, nor had given them any occasion to mention them in their writings, while they were so remote from the sea, and had a conduct of life so peculiar to themselves?

13. Let us now put the case, therefore, that we made use of this argument concerning the Grecians, in order to prove that their nation was not ancient, because nothing is said of them in our records: would not they laugh at us all, and probably give the same reasons for our silence that I have now alleged, and would produce their neighbor nations as witnesses to their own antiquity? Now the very same thing will I endeavor to do; for I will bring the Egyptians and the Phoenicians as my principal witnesses, because nobody can complain Of their testimony as false, on account that they are known to have borne the greatest ill-will towards us; I mean this as to the Egyptians in general all of them, while of the Phoenicians it is known the Tyrians have been most of all in the same ill disposition towards us: yet do I confess that I cannot say the same of the Chaldeans, since our first leaders and ancestors were derived from them; and they do make mention of us Jews in their records, on account of the kindred there is between us. Now when I shall have made my assertions good, so far as concerns the others, I will demonstrate that some of the Greek writers have made mention of us Jews also, that those who envy us may not have even this pretense for contradicting what I have said about our nation.

14. I shall begin with the writings of the Egyptians; not indeed of those that have written in the Egyptian language, which it is impossible for me to do. But Manetho was a man who was by birth an Egyptian, yet had he made himself master of the Greek learning, as is very evident; for he wrote the history of his own country in the Greek tongue, by translating it, as he saith himself, out of their sacred records; he also finds great fault with Herodotus for his ignorance and false relations of Egyptian affairs. Now this Manetho, in the second book of his Egyptian History, writes concerning us in the following manner. I will set down his very words, as if I were to bring the very man himself into a court for a witness: "There was a king of ours whose name was Timaus. Under him it came to pass, I know not how, that God was averse to us, and there came, after a surprising manner, men of ignoble birth out of the eastern parts, and had boldness enough to make an expedition into our country, and with ease subdued it by force, yet without our hazarding a battle with them. So when they had gotten those that governed us under their power, they afterwards burnt down our cities, and demolished the temples of the gods, and used all the inhabitants after a most barbarous manner; nay, some they slew, and led their children and their wives into slavery. At length they made one of themselves king, whose name was Salatis; he also lived at Memphis, and made both the upper and lower regions pay tribute, and left garrisons in places that were the most proper for them. He chiefly aimed

to secure the eastern parts, as fore-seeing that the Assyrians, who had then the greatest power, would be desirous of that kingdom, and invade them; and as he found in the Saite Nomos, [Sethroite,] a city very proper for this purpose, and which lay upon the Bubastic channel, but with regard to a certain theologic notion was called Avaris, this he rebuilt, and made very strong by the walls he built about it, and by a most numerous garrison of two hundred and forty thousand armed men whom he put into it to keep it. Thither Salatis came in summer time, partly to gather his corn, and pay his soldiers their wages, and partly to exercise his armed men, and thereby to terrify foreigners. When this man had reigned thirteen years, after him reigned another, whose name was Beon, for forty-four years; after him reigned another, called Apachnas, thirty-six years and seven months; after him Apophis reigned sixty-one years, and then Janins fifty years and one month; after all these reigned Assis forty-nine years and two months. And these six were the first rulers among them, who were all along making war with the Egyptians, and were very desirous gradually to destroy them to the very roots. This whole nation was styled Hycsos, that is, Shepherd-kings: for the first syllable Hyc, according to the sacred dialect, denotes a king, as is Sos a shepherd; but this according to the ordinary dialect; and of these is compounded Hycsos: but some say that these people were Arabians." Now in another copy it is said that this word does not denote Kings, but, on the contrary, denotes Captive Shepherds, and this on account of the particle Hyc; for that Hyc, with the aspiration, in the Egyptian tongue again denotes Shepherds, and that expressly also; and this to me seems the more probable opinion, and more agreeable to ancient history. [But Manetho goes on]: "These people, whom we have before named kings, and called shepherds also, and their descendants," as he says, "kept possession of Egypt five hundred and eleven years." After these, he says, "That the kings of Thebais and the other parts of Egypt made an insurrection against the shepherds, and that there a terrible and long war was made between them." He says further, "That under a king, whose name was Alisphragmuthosis, the shepherds were subdued by him, and were indeed driven out of other parts of Egypt, but were shut up in a place that contained ten thousand acres; this place was named Avaris." Manetho says, "That the shepherds built a wall round all this place, which was a large and a strong wall, and this in order to keep all their possessions and their prey within a place of strength, but that Thummosis the son of Alisphragmuthosis made an attempt to take them by force and by siege, with four hundred and eighty thousand men to lie rotund about them, but that, upon his despair of taking the place by that siege, they came to a composition with them, that they should leave Egypt, and go, without any harm to be done to them, whithersoever they would; and that, after this composition was made, they went away with their whole families and effects, not fewer in number than two hundred and forty thousand, and took their journey from Egypt, through the wilderness, for Syria; but that as they were in fear of the Assyrians, who had then the dominion over Asia, they built a city in that country which is now called Judea, and that large enough to contain this great number of men, and called it Jerusalem." [9] Now Manetho, in another book of his, says, "That this nation, thus called Shepherds, were also called Captives, in their sacred books." And this account of his is the truth; for feeding of sheep was the employment of our forefathers in the most ancient ages [10] and as they led such a wandering life in feeding sheep, they were called Shepherds. Nor was it without reason that they were called Captives by the Egyptians, since one of our ancestors, Joseph, told the king of Egypt that he was a captive, and afterward sent for his brethren into Egypt by the king's permission. But as for these matters, I shall make a more exact inquiry about them elsewhere. [11]

15. But now I shall produce the Egyptians as witnesses to the antiquity of our nation. I shall therefore here bring in Manetho again, and what he writes as to the order of the times in this case; and thus he speaks: "When this people or shepherds were gone out of Egypt to Jerusalem, Tethtoosis the king of Egypt, who drove them out, reigned afterward twenty-five years and four months, and then died; after him his son Chebron took the kingdom for thirteen years; after whom came Amenophis, for twenty years and seven months; then came his sister Amesses, for twenty-one years and nine months; after her came Mephres, for twelve years and nine months; after him was Mephramuthosis, for twenty-five years and ten months; after him was Thmosis, for nine years and eight months; after him came Amenophis, for thirty years and ten months; after him came Orus, for thirty-six years and five months; then came his daughter Acenchres, for twelve years and one month; then was her brother Rathotis, for nine years; then was Acencheres, for twelve years and five months; then came another Acencheres, for twelve years and three months; after him Armais, for four years and one month; after him was Ramesses, for one year and four months; after him came Armesses Miammoun, for sixty-six years and two months; after him Amenophis, for nineteen years and six months; after him came Sethosis, and Ramesses, who had an army of horse, and a naval force. This king appointed his brother, Armais, to be his deputy over Egypt." [In another copy it stood thus: "After him came Sethosis, and Ramesses, two brethren, the former of whom had a naval force, and in a hostile manner destroyed those that met him upon the sea; but as he slew Ramesses in no long time afterward, so he appointed another of his brethren to be his deputy over Egypt.] He also gave him all the other authority of a king, but

with these only injunctions, that he should not wear the diadem, nor be injurious to the queen, the mother of his children, and that he should not meddle with the other concubines of the king; while he made an expedition against Cyprus, and Phoenicia, and besides against the Assyrians and the Medes. He then subdued them all, some by his arms, some without fighting, and some by the terror of his great army; and being puffed up by the great successes he had had, he went on still the more boldly, and overthrew the cities and countries that lay in the eastern parts. But after some considerable time, Armais, who was left in Egypt, did all those very things, by way of opposition, which his brother had forbid him to do, without fear; for he used violence to the queen, and continued to make use of the rest of the concubines, without sparing any of them; nay, at the persuasion of his friends he put on the diadem, and set up to oppose his brother. But then he who was set over the priests of Egypt wrote letters to Sethosis, and informed him of all that had happened, and how his brother had set up to oppose him: he therefore returned back to Pelusium immediately, and recovered his kingdom again. The country also was called from his name Egypt; for Manetho says, that Sethosis was himself called Egyptus, as was his brother Armais called Danaus."

16. This is Manetho's account. And evident it is from the number of years by him set down belonging to this interval, if they be summed up together, that these shepherds, as they are here called, who were no other than our forefathers, were delivered out of Egypt, and came thence, and inhabited this country, three hundred and ninety-three years before Danaus came to Argos; although the Argives look upon him[12] as their most ancient king Manetho, therefore, hears this testimony to two points of the greatest consequence to our purpose, and those from the Egyptian records themselves. In the first place, that we came out of another country into Egypt; and that withal our deliverance out of it was so ancient in time as to have preceded the siege of Troy almost a thousand years; but then, as to those things which Manetho adds, not from the Egyptian records, but, as he confesses himself, from some stories of an uncertain original, I will disprove them hereafter particularly, and shall demonstrate that they are no better than incredible fables.

17. I will now, therefore, pass from these records, and come to those that belong to the Phoenicians, and concern our nation, and shall produce attestations to what I have said out of them. There are then records among the Tyrians that take in the history of many years, and these are public writings, and are kept with great exactness, and include accounts of the facts done among them, and such as concern their transactions with other nations also, those I mean which were worth remembering. Therein it was recorded that the temple was built by king Solomon

at Jerusalem, one hundred forty-three years and eight months before the Tyrians built Carthage; and in their annals the building of our temple is related; for Hirom, the king of Tyre, was the friend of Solomon our king, and had such friendship transmitted down to him from his forefathers. He thereupon was ambitious to contribute to the splendor of this edifice of Solomon, and made him a present of one hundred and twenty talents of gold. He also cut down the most excellent timber out of that mountain which is called Libanus, and sent it to him for adorning its roof. Solomon also not only made him many other presents, by way of requital, but gave him a country in Galilee also, that was called Chabulon.

[13] But there was another passion, a philosophic inclination of theirs, which cemented the friendship that was betwixt them; for they sent mutual problems to one another, with a desire to have them unriddled by each other; wherein Solomon was superior to Hirom, as he was wiser than he in other respects: and many of the epistles that passed between them are still preserved among the Tyrians. Now, that this may not depend on my bare word, I will produce for a witness Dius, one that is believed to have written the Phoenician History after an accurate manner. This Dius, therefore, writes thus, in his Histories of the Phoenicians: "Upon the death of Abibalus, his son Hirom took the kingdom. This king raised banks at the eastern parts of the city, and enlarged it; he also joined the temple of Jupiter Olympius, which stood before in an island by itself, to the city, by raising a causeway between them, and adorned that temple with donations of gold. He moreover went up to Libanus, and had timber cut down for the building of temples. They say further, that Solomon, when he was king of Jerusalem, sent problems to Hirom to be solved, and desired he would send others back for him to solve, and that he who could not solve the problems proposed to him should pay money to him that solved them. And when Hirom had agreed to the proposals, but was not able to solve the problems, he was obliged to pay a great deal of money, as a penalty for the same. As also they relate, that one OEabdemon, a man of Tyre, did solve the problems, and propose others which Solomon could not solve, upon which he was obliged to repay a great deal of money to Hirom." These things are attested to by Dius, and confirm what we have said upon the same subjects before.

18. And now I shall add Menander the Ephesian, as an additional witness. This Menander wrote the Acts that were done both by the Greeks and Barbarians, under every one of the Tyrian kings, and had taken much pains to learn their history out of their own records. Now when he was writing about those kings that had reigned at Tyre, he came to Hirom, and says thus: "Upon the death of Abibalus, his son Hirom took the kingdom; he lived fifty-three years, and reigned

thirty-four. He raised a bank on that called the Broad Place, and dedicated that golden pillar which is in Jupiter's temple; he also went and cut down timber from the mountain called Libanus, and got timber Of cedar for the roofs of the temples. He also pulled down the old temples, and built new ones; besides this, he consecrated the temples of Hercules and of Astarte. He first built Hercules's temple in the month Peritus, and that of Astarte when he made his expedition against the Tityans, who would not pay him their tribute; and when he had subdued them to himself, he returned home. Under this king there was a younger son of Abdemon, who mastered the problems which Solomon king of Jerusalem had recommended to be solved." Now the time from this king to the building of Carthage is thus calculated: "Upon the death of Hirom, Baleazarus his son took the kingdom; he lived forty-three years, and reigned seven years: after him succeeded his son Abdastartus; he lived twenty-nine years, and reigned nine years. Now four sons of his nurse plotted against him and slew him, the eldest of whom reigned twelve years: after them came Astartus, the son of Deleastartus; he lived fifty-four years, and reigned twelve years: after him came his brother Aserymus; he lived fifty-four years, and reigned nine years: he was slain by his brother Pheles, who took the kingdom and reigned but eight months, though he lived fifty years: he was slain by Ithobalus, the priest of Astarte, who reigned thirty-two years, and lived sixty-eight years: he was succeeded by his son Badezorus, who lived forty-five years, and reigned six years: he was succeeded by Matgenus his son; he lived thirty-two years, and reigned nine years: Pygmalion succeeded him; he lived fifty-six years, and reigned forty-seven years. Now in the seventh year of his reign, his sister fled away from him, and built the city Carthage in Libya." So the whole time from the reign of Hirom, till the building of Carthage, amounts to the sum of one hundred fifty-five years and eight months. Since then the temple was built at Jerusalem in the twelfth year of the reign of Hirom, there were from the building of the temple, until the building of Carthage, one hundred forty-three years and eight months. Wherefore, what occasion is there for alleging any more testimonies out of the Phoenician histories [on the behalf of our nation], since what I have said is so thoroughly confirmed already? and to be sure our ancestors came into this country long before the building of the temple; for it was not till we had gotten possession of the whole land by war that we built our temple. And this is the point that I have clearly proved out of our sacred writings in my Antiquities.

19. I will now relate what hath been written concerning us in the Chaldean histories, which records have a great agreement with our books in oilier things also. Berosus shall be witness to what I say: he was by birth a Chaldean, well known by the learned, on account of his publication of the Chaldean books of

astronomy and philosophy among the Greeks. This Berosus, therefore, following the most ancient records of that nation, gives us a history of the deluge of waters that then happened, and of the destruction of mankind thereby, and agrees with Moses's narration thereof. He also gives us an account of that ark wherein Noah, the origin of our race, was preserved, when it was brought to the highest part of the Armenian mountains; after which he gives us a catalogue of the posterity of Noah, and adds the years of their chronology, and at length comes down to Nabolassar, who was king of Babylon, and of the Chaldeans. And when he was relating the acts of this king, he describes to us how he sent his son Nabuchodonosor against Egypt, and against our land, with a great army, upon his being informed that they had revolted from him; and how, by that means, he subdued them all, and set our temple that was at Jerusalem on fire; nay, and removed our people entirely out of their own country, and transferred them to Babylon; when it so happened that our city was desolate during the interval of seventy years, until the days of Cyrus king of Persia. He then says, "That this Babylonian king conquered Egypt, and Syria, and Phoenicia, and Arabia, and exceeded in his exploits all that had reigned before him in Babylon and Chaldea." A little after which Berosus subjoins what follows in his History of Ancient Times. I will set down Berosus's own accounts, which are these: "When Nabolassar, father of Nabuchodonosor, heard that the governor whom he had set over Egypt, and over the parts of Celesyria and Phoenicia, had revolted from him, he was not able to bear it any longer; but committing certain parts of his army to his son Nabuchodonosor, who was then but young, he sent him against the rebel: Nabuchodonosor joined battle with him, and conquered him, and reduced the country under his dominion again. Now it so fell out that his father Nabolassar fell into a distemper at this time, and died in the city of Babylon, after he had reigned twenty-nine years. But as he understood, in a little time, that his father Nabolassar was dead, he set the affairs of Egypt and the other countries in order, and committed the captives he had taken from the Jews, and Phoenicians, and Syrians, and of the nations belonging to Egypt, to some of his friends, that they might conduct that part of the forces that had on heavy armor, with the rest of his baggage, to Babylonia; while he went in haste, having but a few with him, over the desert to Babylon; whither, when he was come, he found the public affairs had been managed by the Chaldeans, and that the principal person among them had preserved the kingdom for him. Accordingly, he now entirely obtained all his father's dominions. He then came, and ordered the captives to be placed as colonies in the most proper places of Babylonia; but for himself, he adorned the temple of Belus, and the other temples, after an elegant manner, out of the spoils he had taken in this war. He also rebuilt the old city, and added another to it on the outside, and so far restored Babylon, that none who should besiege it afterwards might have it in their power to divert the river, so as to facilitate an entrance into it; and this he did by building three walls about the inner city, and three about the outer. Some of these walls he built of burnt brick and bitumen, and some of brick only. So when he had thus fortified the city with walls, after an excellent manner, and had adorned the gates magnificently, he added a new palace to that which his father had dwelt in, and this close by it also, and that more eminent in its height, and in its great splendor. It would perhaps require too long a narration, if any one were to describe it. However, as prodigiously large and as magnificent as it was, it was finished in fifteen days. Now in this palace he erected very high walks, supported by stone pillars, and by planting what was called a pensile paradise, and replenishing it with all sorts of trees, he rendered the prospect an exact resemblance of a mountainous country. This he did to please his queen, because she had been brought up in Media, and was fond of a mountainous situation."

20. This is what Berosus relates concerning the forementioned king, as he relates many other things about him also in the third book of his Chaldean History; wherein he complains of the Grecian writers for supposing, without any foundation, that Babylon was built by Semiramis, [14] queen of Assyria, and for her false pretense to those wonderful edifices thereto buildings at Babylon, do no way contradict those ancient and relating, as if they were her own workmanship; as indeed in these affairs the Chaldean History cannot but be the most credible. Moreover, we meet with a confirmation of what Berosus says in the archives of the Phoenicians, concerning this king Nabuchodonosor, that he conquered all Syria and Phoenicia; in which case Philostratus agrees with the others in that history which he composed, where he mentions the siege of Tyre; as does Megasthenes also, in the fourth book of his Indian History, wherein he pretends to prove that the forementioned king of the Babylonians was superior to Hercules in strength and the greatness of his exploits; for he says that he conquered a great part of Libya, and conquered Iberia also. Now as to what I have said before about the temple at Jerusalem, that it was fought against by the Babylonians, and burnt by them, but was opened again when Cyrus had taken the kingdom of Asia, shall now be demonstrated from what Berosus adds further upon that head; for thus he says in his third book: "Nabuchodonosor, after he had begun to build the forementioned wall, fell sick, and departed this life, when he had reigned forty-three years; whereupon his son Evilmerodach obtained the kingdom. He governed public affairs after an illegal and impure manner, and had a plot laid

against him by Neriglissoor, his sister's husband, and was slain by him when he had reigned but two years. After he was slain, Neriglissoor, the person who plotted against him, succeeded him in the kingdom, and reigned four years; his son Laborosoarchod obtained the kingdom, though he was but a child, and kept it nine months; but by reason of the very ill temper and ill practices he exhibited to the world, a plot was laid against him also by his friends, and he was tormented to death. After his death, the conspirators got together, and by common consent put the crown upon the head of Nabonnedus, a man of Babylon, and one who belonged to that insurrection. In his reign it was that the walls of the city of Babylon were curiously built with burnt brick and bitumen; but when he was come to the seventeenth year of his reign, Cyrus came out of Persia with a great army; and having already conquered all the rest of Asia, he came hastily to Babylonia. When Nabonnedus perceived he was coming to attack him, he met him with his forces, and joining battle with him was beaten, and fled away with a few of his troops with him, and was shut up within the city Borsippus. Hereupon Cyrus took Babylon, and gave order that the outer walls of the city should be demolished, because the city had proved very troublesome to him, and cost him a great deal of pains to take it. He then marched away to Borsippus, to besiege Nabonnedus; but as Nabonnedus did not sustain the siege, but delivered himself into his hands, he was at first kindly used by Cyrus, who gave him Carmania, as a place for him to inhabit in, but sent him out of Babylonia. Accordingly Nabonnedus spent the rest of his time in that country, and there died."

21. These accounts agree with the true histories in our books; for in them it is written that Nebuchadnezzar, in the eighteenth year of his reign, laid our temple desolate, and so it lay in that state of obscurity for fifty years; but that in the second year of the reign of Cyrus its foundations were laid, and it was finished again in the second year of Darius. I will now add the records of the Phoenicians; for it will not be superfluous to give the reader demonstrations more than enough on this occasion. In them we have this enumeration of the times of their several kings: "Nabuchodonosor besieged Tyre for thirteen years in the days of Ithobal, their king; after him reigned Baal, ten years; after him were judges appointed, who judged the people: Ecnibalus, the son of Baslacus, two months; Chelbes, the son of Abdeus, ten months; Abbar, the high priest, three months; Mitgonus and Gerastratus, the sons of Abdelemus, were judges six years; after whom Balatorus reigned one year; after his death they sent and fetched Merbalus from Babylon, who reigned four years; after his death they sent for his brother Hirom, who reigned twenty years. Under his reign Cyrus became king of Persia." So that the

whole interval is fifty-four years besides three months; for in the seventh year of the reign of Nebuchadnezzar he began to besiege Tyre, and Cyrus the Persian took the kingdom in the fourteenth year of Hirom. So that the records of the Chaldeans and Tyrians agree with our writings about this temple; and the testimonies here produced are an indisputable and undeniable attestation to the antiquity of our nation. And I suppose that what I have already said may be sufficient to such as are not very contentious.

22. But now it is proper to satisfy the inquiry of those that disbelieve the records of barbarians, and think none but Greeks to be worthy of credit, and to produce many of these very Greeks who were acquainted with our nation, and to set before them such as upon occasion have made mention of us in their own writings. Pythagoras, therefore, of Samos, lived in very ancient times, and was esteemed a person superior to all philosophers in wisdom and piety towards God. Now it is plain that he did not only know our doctrines, but was in very great measure a follower and admirer of them. There is not indeed extant any writing that is owned for his [15] but many there are who have written his history, of whom Hermippus is the most celebrated, who was a person very inquisitive into all sorts of history. Now this Hermippus, in his first book concerning Pythagoras, speaks thus: "That Pythagoras, upon the death of one of his associates, whose name was Calliphon, a Crotonlate by birth, affirmed that this man's soul conversed with him both night and day, and enjoined him not to pass over a place where an ass had fallen down; as also not to drink of such waters as caused thirst again; and to abstain from all sorts of reproaches." After which he adds thus: "This he did and said in imitation of the doctrines of the Jews and Thracians, which he transferred into his own philosophy." For it is very truly affirmed of this Pythagoras, that he took a great many of the laws of the Jews into his own philosophy. Nor was our nation unknown of old to several of the Grecian cities, and indeed was thought worthy of imitation by some of them. This is declared by Theophrastus, in his writings concerning laws; for he says that "the laws of the Tyrians forbid men to swear foreign oaths." Among which he enumerates some others, and particularly that called Corban: which oath can only be found among the Jews, and declares what a man may call "A thing devoted to God." Nor indeed was Herodotus of Halicarnassus unacquainted with our nation, but mentions it after a way of his own, when he saith thus, in the second book concerning the Colchians. His words are these: "The only people who were circumcised in their privy members originally, were the Colchians, the Egyptians, and the Ethiopians; but the Phoenicians and those Syrians that are in Palestine confess that they learned it from the Egyptians. And for those Syrians who live about the rivers Thermodon

and Parthenius, and their neighbors the Macrones, they say they have lately learned it from the Colchians; for these are the only people that are circumcised among mankind, and appear to have done the very same thing with the Egyptians. But as for the Egyptians and Ethiopians themselves, I am not able to say which of them received it from the other." This therefore is what Herodotus says, that "the Syrians that are in Palestine are circumcised." But there are no inhabitants of Palestine that are circumcised excepting the Jews; and therefore it must be his knowledge of them that enabled him to speak so much concerning them. Cherilus also, a still ancienter writer, and a poet, [16] makes mention of our nation, and informs us that it came to the assistance of king Xerxes, in his expedition against Greece. For in his enumeration of all those nations, he last of all inserts ours among the rest, when he says, "At the last there passed over a people, wonderful to be beheld; for they spake the Phoenician tongue with their mouths; they dwelt in the Solymean mountains, near a broad lake: their heads were sooty; they had round rasures on them; their heads and faces were like nasty horse-heads also, that had been hardened in the smoke." I think, therefore, that it is evident to every body that Cherilus means us, because the Solymean mountains are in our country, wherein we inhabit, as is also the lake called Asphaltitis; for this is a broader and larger lake than any other that is in Syria: and thus does Cherilus make mention of us. But now that not only the lowest sort of the Grecians, but those that are had in the greatest admiration for their philosophic improvements among them, did not only know the Jews, but when they lighted upon any of them, admired them also, it is easy for any one to know. For Clearchus, who was the scholar of Aristotle, and inferior to no one of the Peripatetics whomsoever, in his first book concerning sleep, says that "Aristotle his master related what follows of a Jew," and sets down Aristotle's own discourse with him. The account is this, as written down by him: "Now, for a great part of what this Jew said, it would be too long to recite it; but what includes in it both wonder and philosophy it may not be amiss to discourse of. Now, that I may be plain with thee, Hyperochides, I shall herein seem to thee to relate wonders, and what will resemble dreams themselves. Hereupon Hyperochides answered modestly, and said, For that very reason it is that all of us are very desirous of hearing what thou art going to say. Then replied Aristotle, For this cause it will be the best way to imitate that rule of the Rhetoricians, which requires us first to give an account of the man, and of what nation he was, that so we may not contradict our master's directions. Then said Hyperochides, Go on, if it so pleases thee. This man then, [answered Aristotle,] was by birth a Jew, and came from Celesyria; these Jews are derived from the Indian philosophers; they are named by the Indians Calami, and by the Syrians

Judaei, and took their name from the country they inhabit, which is called Judea; but for the name of their city, it is a very awkward one, for they call it Jerusalem. Now this man, when he was hospitably treated by a great many, came down from the upper country to the places near the sea, and became a Grecian, not only in his language, but in his soul also; insomuch that when we ourselves happened to be in Asia about the same places whither he came, he conversed with us, and with other philosophical persons, and made a trial of our skill in philosophy; and as he had lived with many learned men, he communicated to us more information than he received from us." This is Aristotle's account of the matter, as given us by Clearchus; which Aristotle discoursed also particularly of the great and wonderful fortitude of this Jew in his diet, and continent way of living, as those that please may learn more about him from Clearchus's book itself; for I avoid setting down any more than is sufficient for my purpose. Now Clearchus said this by way of digression, for his main design was of another nature. But for Hecateus of Abdera, who was both a philosopher, and one very useful ill an active life, he was contemporary with king Alexander in his youth, and afterward was with Ptolemy, the son of Lagus; he did not write about the Jewish affairs by the by only, but composed an entire book concerning the Jews themselves; out of which book I am willing to run over a few things, of which I have been treating by way of epitome. And, in the first place, I will demonstrate the time when this Hecateus lived; for he mentions the fight that was between Ptolemy and Demetrius about Gaza, which was fought in the eleventh year after the death of Alexander, and in the hundred and seventeenth olympiad, as Castor says in his history. For when he had set down this olympiad, he says further, that "in this olympiad Ptolemy, the son of Lagus, beat in battle Demetrius, the son of Antigonus, who was named Poliorcetes, at Gaza." Now, it is agreed by all, that Alexander died in the hundred and fourteenth olympiad; it is therefore evident that our nation flourished in his time, and in the time of Alexander. Again, Hecateus says to the same purpose, as follows: "Ptolemy got possession of the places in Syria after that battle at Gaza; and many, when they heard of Ptolemy's moderation and humanity, went along with him to Egypt, and were willing to assist him in his affairs; one of whom [Hecateus says] was Hezekiah [17] the high priest of the Jews; a man of about sixty-six years of age, and in great dignity among his own people. He was a very sensible man, and could speak very movingly, and was very skillful in the management of affairs, if any other man ever were so; although, as he says, all the priests of the Jews took tithes of the products of the earth, and managed public affairs, and were in number not above fifteen hundred at the most." Hecateus mentions this Hezekiah a second time, and says, that "as he was possessed of so great a dignity, and was become familiar with us, so did he take certain of those that were with him, and explained to them all the circumstances of their people; for he had all their habitations and polity down in writing." Moreover, Hecateus declares again, "what regard we have for our laws, and that we resolve to endure any thing rather than transgress them, because we think it right for us to do so." Whereupon he adds, that "although they are in a bad reputation among their neighbors, and among all those that come to them, and have been often treated injuriously by the kings and governors of Persia, yet can they not be dissuaded from acting what they think best; but that when they are stripped on this account, and have torments inflicted upon them, and they are brought to the most terrible kinds of death, they meet them after an extraordinary manner, beyond all other people, and will not renounce the religion of their forefathers." Hecateus also produces demonstrations not a few of this their resolute tenaciousness of their laws, when he speaks thus: "Alexander was once at Babylon, and had an intention to rebuild the temple of Belus that was fallen to decay, and in order thereto, he commanded all his soldiers in general to bring earth thither. But the Jews, and they only, would not comply with that command; nay, they underwent stripes and great losses of what they had on this account, till the king forgave them, and permitted them to live in quiet." He adds further, that "when the Macedonians came to them into that country, and demolished the [old] temples and the altars, they assisted them in demolishing them all [18] but [for not assisting them in rebuilding them] they either underwent losses, or sometimes obtained forgiveness." He adds further, that "these men deserve to be admired on that account." He also speaks of the mighty populousness of our nation, and says that "the Persians formerly carried away many ten thousands of our people to Babylon, as also that not a few ten thousands were removed after Alexander's death into Egypt and Phoenicia, by reason of the sedition that was arisen in Syria." The same person takes notice in his history, how large the country is which we inhabit, as well as of its excellent character, and says, that "the land in which the Jews inhabit contains three millions of arourae,[19] and is generally of a most excellent and most fruitful soil; nor is Judea of lesser dimensions." The same man describe our city Jerusalem also itself as of a most excellent structure, and very large, and inhabited from the most ancient times. He also discourses of the multitude of men in it, and of the construction of our temple, after the following manner: "There are many strong places and villages [says he] in the country of Judea; but one strong city there is, about fifty furlongs in circumference, which is inhabited by a hundred and twenty thousand men, or thereabouts; they call it Jerusalem. There is about the middle of the city a wall of stone, whose length is five hundred feet, and the breadth a hundred cubits, with double cloisters; wherein there is a square altar, not made of hewn stone, but composed of white stones gathered together, having each side twenty cubits long, and its altitude ten cubits. Hard by it is a large edifice, wherein there is an altar and a candlestick, both of gold, and in weight two talents: upon these there is a light that is never extinguished, either by night or by day. There is no image, nor any thing, nor any donations therein; nothing at all is there planted, neither grove, nor any thing of that sort. The priests abide therein both nights and days, performing certain purifications, and drinking not the least drop of wine while they are in the temple." Moreover, he attests that we Jews went as auxiliaries along with king Alexander, and after him with his successors. I will add further what he says he learned when he was himself with the same army, concerning the actions of a man that was a Jew. His words are these: "As I was myself going to the Red Sea, there followed us a man, whose name was Mosollam; he was one of the Jewish horsemen who conducted us; he was a person of great courage, of a strong body, and by all allowed to be the most skillful archer that was either among the Greeks or barbarians. Now this man, as people were in great numbers passing along the road, and a certain augur was observing an augury by a bird, and requiring them all to stand still, inquired what they staid for. Hereupon the augur showed him the bird from whence he took his augury, and told him that if the bird staid where he was, they ought all to stand still; but that if he got up, and flew onward, they must go forward; but that if he flew backward, they must retire again. Mosollam made no reply, but drew his bow, and shot at the bird, and hit him, and killed him; and as the augur and some others were very angry, and wished imprecations upon him, he answered them thus: Why are you so mad as to take this most unhappy bird into your hands? for how can this bird give us any true information concerning our march, who could not foresee how to save himself? for had he been able to foreknow what was future, he would not have come to this place, but would have been afraid lest Mosollam the Jew should shoot at him, and kill him." But of Hecateus's testimonies we have said enough; for as to such as desire to know more of them, they may easily obtain them from his book itself. However, I shall not think it too much for me to name Agatharchides, as having made mention of us Jews, though in way of derision at our simplicity, as he supposes it to be; for when he was discoursing of the affairs of Stratonice, "how she came out of Macedonia into Syria, and left her husband Demetrius, while yet Seleueus would not marry her as she expected, but during the time of his raising an army at Babylon, stirred up a sedition about Antioch; and how, after that, the king came back, and upon his taking of Antioch, she fled to Seleucia, and had it in her power to sail away immediately yet did she comply with a dream which forbade her so to do, and so was caught and put to death." When Agatharchides had premised this story, and had jested upon Stratonice for her superstition, he gives a like example of what was reported concerning us, and writes thus: "There are a people called Jews, and dwell in a city the strongest of all other cities, which the inhabitants call Jerusalem, and are accustomed to rest on every seventh day [20] on which times they make no use of their arms, nor meddle with husbandry, nor take care of any affairs of life, but spread out their hands in their holy places, and pray till the evening. Now it came to pass, that when Ptolemy, the son of Lagus, came into this city with his army, that these men, in observing this mad custom of theirs, instead of guarding the city, suffered their country to submit itself to a bitter lord; and their law was openly proved to have commanded a foolish practice. [21] This accident taught all other men but the Jews to disregard such dreams as these were, and not to follow the like idle suggestions delivered as a law, when, in such uncertainty of human reasonings, they are at a loss what they should do." Now this our procedure seems a ridiculous thing to Agatharchides, but will appear to such as consider it without prejudice a great thing, and what deserved a great many encomiums; I mean, when certain men constantly prefer the observation of their laws, and their religion towards God, before the preservation of themselves and their country.

23. Now that some writers have omitted to mention our nation, not because they knew nothing of us, but because they envied us, or for some other unjustifiable reasons, I think I can demonstrate by particular instances; for Hieronymus, who wrote the History of Alexander's Successors, lived at the same time with Hecateus, and was a friend of king Antigonus, and president of Syria. Now it is plain that Hecateus wrote an entire book concerning us, while Hieronymus never mentions us in his history, although he was bred up very near to the places where we live. Thus different from one another are the inclinations of men; while the one thought we deserved to be carefully remembered, as some ill-disposed passion blinded the other's mind so entirely, that he could not discern the truth. And now certainly the foregoing records of the Egyptians, and Chaldeans, and Phoenicians, together with so many of the Greek writers, will be sufficient for the demonstration of our antiquity. Moreover, besides those forementioned, Theophilus, and Theodotus, and Mnaseas, and Aristophanes, and Hermogenes, Euhemerus also, and Conon, and Zopyrion, and perhaps many others, [for I have not lighted upon all the Greek books,] have made distinct mention of us. It is true, many of the men before mentioned have made great mistakes about the true accounts of our nation in the earliest times, because they had not perused our sacred books; yet have they all of them afforded their

testimony to our antiquity, concerning which I am now treating. However, Demetrius Phalereus, and the elder Philo, with Eupolemus, have not greatly missed the truth about our affairs; whose lesser mistakes ought therefore to be forgiven them; for it was not in their power to understand our writings with the utmost accuracy.

24. One particular there is still remaining behind of what I at first proposed to speak to, and that is, to demonstrate that those calumnies and reproaches which some have thrown upon our nation, are lies, and to make use of those writers' own testimonies against themselves; and that in general this self-contradiction hath happened to many other authors by reason of their ill-will to some people, I conclude, is not unknown to such as have read histories with sufficient care; for some of them have endeavored to disgrace the nobility of certain nations, and of some of the most glorious cities, and have cast reproaches upon certain forms of government. Thus hath Theopompus abused the city of Athens, Polycrates that of Lacedemon, as hath he hat wrote the Tripoliticus [for he is not Theopompus, as is supposed by some] done by the city of Thebes. Timeils also hath greatly abused the foregoing people and others also; and this ill-treatment they use chiefly when they have a contest with men of the greatest reputation; some out of envy and malice, and others as supposing that by this foolish talking of theirs they may be thought worthy of being remembered themselves; and indeed they do by no means fail of their hopes, with regard to the foolish part of mankind, but men of sober judgment still condemn them of great malignity.

25. Now the Egyptians were the first that cast reproaches upon us; in order to please which nation, some others undertook to pervert the truth, while they would neither own that our forefathers came into Egypt from another country, as the fact was, nor give a true account of our departure thence. And indeed the Egyptians took many occasions to hate us and envy us: in the first place, because our ancestors had had the dominion over their country? and when they were delivered from them, and gone to their own country again, they lived there in prosperity. In the next place, the difference of our religion from theirs hath occasioned great enmity between us, while our way of Divine worship did as much exceed that which their laws appointed, as does the nature of God exceed that of brute beasts; for so far they all agree through the whole country, to esteem such animals as gods, although they differ one from another in the peculiar worship they severally pay to them. And certainly men they are entirely of vain and foolish minds, who have thus accustomed themselves from the beginning to have such bad notions concerning their gods, and could not think of imitating that decent form of

Divine worship which we made use of, though, when they saw our institutions approved of by many others, they could not but envy us on that account; for some of them have proceeded to that degree of folly and meanness in their conduct, as not to scruple to contradict their own ancient records, nay, to contradict themselves also in their writings, and yet were so blinded by their passions as not to discern it.

26. And now I will turn my discourse to one of their principal writers, whom I have a little before made use of as a witness to our antiquity; I mean Manetho.[22] He promised to interpret the Egyptian history out of their sacred writings, and premised this: that "our people had come into Egypt, many ten thousands in number, and subdued its inhabitants;" and when he had further confessed that "we went out of that country afterward, and settled in that country which is now called Judea, and there built Jerusalem and its temple." Now thus far he followed his ancient records; but after this he permits himself, in order to appear to have written what rumors and reports passed abroad about the Jews, and introduces incredible narrations, as if he would have the Egyptian multitude, that had the leprosy and other distempers, to have been mixed with us, as he says they were, and that they were condemned to fly out of Egypt together; for he mentions Amenophis, a fictitious king's name, though on that account he durst not set down the number of years of his reign, which yet he had accurately done as to the other kings he mentions; he then ascribes certain fabulous stories to this king, as having in a manner forgotten how he had already related that the departure of the shepherds for Jerusalem had been five hundred and eighteen years before; for Tethmosis was king when they went away. Now, from his days, the reigns of the intermediate kings, according to Manethe, amounted to three hundred and ninety-three years, as he says himself, till the two brothers Sethos and Hermeus; the one of whom, Sethos, was called by that other name of Egyptus, and the other, Hermeus, by that of Danaus. He also says that Sethos east the other out of Egypt, and reigned fifty-nine years, as did his eldest son Rhampses reign after him sixty-six years. When Manethe therefore had acknowledged that our forefathers were gone out of Egypt so many years ago, he introduces his fictitious king Amenophis, and says thus: "This king was desirous to become a spectator of the gods, as had Orus, one of his predecessors in that kingdom, desired the same before him; he also communicated that his desire to his namesake Amenophis, who was the son of Papis, and one that seemed to partake of a divine nature, both as to wisdom and the knowledge of futurities." Manethe adds, "how this namesake of his told him that he might see the gods, if he would clear the whole country of the lepers and of the other impure people; that the king was pleased with this injunction, and got

together all that had any defect in their bodies out of Egypt; and that their number was eighty thousand; whom he sent to those quarries which are on the east side of the Nile, that they might work in them, and might be separated from the rest of the Egyptians." He says further, that "there were some of the learned priests that were polluted with the leprosy; but that still this Amenophis, the wise man and the prophet, was afraid that the gods would be angry at him and at the king, if there should appear to have been violence offered them; who also added this further, [out of his sagacity about futurities,] that certain people would come to the assistance of these polluted wretches, and would conquer Egypt, and keep it in their possession thirteen years; that, however, he durst not tell the king of these things, but that he left a writing behind him about all those matters, and then slew himself, which made the king disconsolate." After which he writes thus verbatim: "After those that were sent to work in the quarries had continued in that miserable state for a long while, the king was desired that he would set apart the city Avaris, which was then left desolate of the shepherds, for their habitation and protection; which desire he granted them. Now this city, according to the ancient theology, was Typho's city. But when these men were gotten into it, and found the place fit for a revolt, they appointed themselves a ruler out of the priests of Hellopolis, whose name was Osarsiph, and they took their oaths that they would be obedient to him in all things. He then, in the first place, made this law for them, That they should neither worship the Egyptian gods, nor should abstain from any one of those sacred animals which they have in the highest esteem, but kill and destroy them all; that they should join themselves to nobody but to those that were of this confederacy. When he had made such laws as these, and many more such as were mainly opposite to the customs of the Egyptians, [23] he gave order that they should use the multitude of the hands they had in building walls about their City, and make themselves ready for a war with king Amenophis, while he did himself take into his friendship the other priests, and those that were polluted with them, and sent ambassadors to those shepherds who had been driven out of the land by Tefilmosis to the city called Jerusalem; whereby he informed them of his own affairs, and of the state of those others that had been treated after such an ignominious manner, and desired that they would come with one consent to his assistance in this war against Egypt. He also promised that he would, in the first place, bring them back to their ancient city and country Avaris, and provide a plentiful maintenance for their multitude; that he would protect them and fight for them as occasion should require, and would easily reduce the country under their dominion. These shepherds were all very glad of this message, and came away with alacrity all together, being in number two hundred thousand men; and in a little time they came to Avaris. And now Amenophis the king of Egypt, upon his being informed of their invasion, was in great confusion, as calling to mind what Amenophis, the son of Papis, had foretold him; and, in the first place, he assembled the multitude of the Egyptians, and took counsel with their leaders, and sent for their sacred animals to him, especially for those that were principally worshipped in their temples, and gave a particular charge to the priests distinctly, that they should hide the images of their gods with the utmost care he also sent his son Sethos, who was also named Ramesses, from his father Rhampses, being but five years old, to a friend of his. He then passed on with the rest of the Egyptians, being three hundred thousand of the most warlike of them, against the enemy, who met them. Yet did he not join battle with them; but thinking that would be to fight against the gods, he returned back and came to Memphis, where he took Apis and the other sacred animals which he had sent for to him, and presently marched into Ethiopia, together with his whole army and multitude of Egyptians; for the king of Ethiopia was under an obligation to him, on which account he received him, and took care of all the multitude that was with him, while the country supplied all that was necessary for the food of the men. He also allotted cities and villages for this exile, that was to be from its beginning during those fatally determined thirteen years. Moreover, he pitched a camp for his Ethiopian army, as a guard to king Amenophis, upon the borders of Egypt. And this was the state of things in Ethiopia. But for the people of Jerusalem, when they came down together with the polluted Egyptians, they treated the men in such a barbarous manner, that those who saw how they subdued the forementioned country, and the horrid wickedness they were guilty of, thought it a most dreadful thing; for they did not only set the cities and villages on fire but were not satisfied till they had been guilty of sacrilege, and destroyed the images of the gods, and used them in roasting those sacred animals that used to be worshipped, and forced the priests and prophets to be the executioners and murderers of those animals, and then ejected them naked out of the country. It was also reported that the priest, who ordained their polity and their laws, was by birth of Hellopolls, and his name Osarsiph, from Osyris, who was the god of Hellopolls; but that when he was gone over to these people, his name was changed, and he was called Moses."

27. This is what the Egyptians relate about the Jews, with much more, which I omit for the sake of brevity. But still Manetho goes on, that "after this, Amenophis returned back from Ethiopia with a great army, as did his son Ahampses with another army also, and that both of them joined battle with the shepherds and the polluted people, and beat them, and slew a great many of

them, and pursued them to the bounds of Syria." These and the like accounts are written by Manetho. But I will demonstrate that he trifles, and tells arrant lies, after I have made a distinction which will relate to what I am going to say about him; for this Manetho had granted and confessed that this nation was not originally Egyptian, but that they had come from another country, and subdued Egypt, and then went away again out of it. But that those Egyptians who were thus diseased in their bodies were not mingled with us afterward, and that Moses who brought the people out was not one of that company, but lived many generations earlier, I shall endeavor to demonstrate from Manetho's own accounts themselves.

28. Now, for the first occasion of this fiction, Manetho supposes what is no better than a ridiculous thing; for he says that, "King Amenophis desired to see the gods." What gods, I pray, did he desire to see? If he meant the gods whom their laws ordained to be worshipped, the ox, the goat, the crocodile, and the baboon, he saw them already; but for the heavenly gods, how could he see them, and what should occasion this his desire? To be sure? it was because another king before him had already seen them. He had then been informed what sort of gods they were, and after what manner they had been seen, insomuch that he did not stand in need of any new artifice for obtaining this sight. However, the prophet by whose means the king thought to compass his design was a wise man. If so, how came he not to know that such his desire was impossible to be accomplished? for the event did not succeed. And what pretense could there be to suppose that the gods would not be seen by reason of the people's maims in their bodies, or leprosy? for the gods are not angry at the imperfection of bodies, but at wicked practices; and as to eighty thousand lepers, and those in an ill state also, how is it possible to have them gathered together in one day? nay, how came the king not to comply with the prophet? for his injunction was, that those that were maimed should be expelled out of Egypt, while the king only sent them to work in the quarries, as if he were rather in want of laborers, than intended to purge his country. He says further, that, "this prophet slew himself, as foreseeing the anger of the gods, and those events which were to come upon Egypt afterward; and that he left this prediction for the king in writing." Besides, how came it to pass that this prophet did not foreknow his own death at the first? nay, how came he not to contradict the king in his desire to see the gods immediately? how came that unreasonable dread upon him of judgments that were not to happen in his lifetime? or what worse thing could he suffer, out of the fear of which he made haste to kill himself? But now let us see the silliest thing of all:—The king, although he had been informed of these things, and terrified with the fear of what was to come, yet did not he even then eject these maimed people out of his country,

when it had been foretold him that he was to clear Egypt of them; but, as Manetho says, "he then, upon their request, gave them that city to inhabit, which had formerly belonged to the shepherds, and was called Avaris; whither when they were gone in crowds," he says, "they chose one that had formerly been priest of Hellopolls; and that this priest first ordained that they should neither worship the gods, nor abstain from those animals that were worshipped by the Egyptians, but should kill and eat them all, and should associate with nobody but those that had conspired with them; and that he bound the multitude by oaths to be sure to continue in those laws; and that when he had built a wall about Avaris, he made war against the king." Manetho adds also, that "this priest sent to Jerusalem to invite that people to come to his assistance, and promised to give them Avaris; for that it had belonged to the forefathers of those that were coming from Jerusalem, and that when they were come, they made a war immediately against the king, and got possession of all Egypt." He says also that "the Egyptians came with an army of two hundred thousand men, and that Amenophis, the king of Egypt, not thinking that he ought to fight against the gods, ran away presently into Ethiopia, and committed Apis and certain other of their sacred animals to the priests, and commanded them to take care of preserving them." He says further, that, "the people of Jerusalem came accordingly upon the Egyptians, and overthrew their cities, and burnt their temples, and slew their horsemen, and, in short, abstained from no sort of wickedness nor barbarity; and for that priest who settled their polity and their laws," he says, "he was by birth of Hellopolis, and his name was Osarsiph, from Osyris the god of Hellopolis, but that he changed his name, and called himself Moses." He then says that "on the thirteenth year afterward, Amenophis, according to the fatal time of the duration of his misfortunes, came upon them out of Ethiopia with a great army, and joining battle with the shepherds and with the polluted people, overcame them in battle, and slew a great many of them, and pursued them as far as the bounds of Syria."

29. Now Manetho does not reflect upon the improbability of his lie; for the leprous people, and the multitude that was with them, although they might formerly have been angry at the king, and at those that had treated them so coarsely, and this according to the prediction of the prophet; yet certainly, when they were come out of the mines, and had received of the king a city, and a country, they would have grown milder towards him. However, had they ever so much hated him in particular, they might have laid a private plot against himself, but would hardly have made war against all the Egyptians; I mean this on the account of the great kindred they who were so numerous must have had among them. Nay still, if they had resolved to fight with the men, they would not have

had impudence enough to fight with their gods; nor would they have ordained laws quite contrary to those of their own country, and to those in which they had been bred up themselves. Yet are we beholden to Manethe, that he does not lay the principal charge of this horrid transgression upon those that came from Jerusalem, but says that the Egyptians themselves were the most guilty, and that they were their priests that contrived these things, and made the multitude take their oaths for doing so. But still how absurd is it to suppose that none of these people's own relations or friends should be prevailed with to revolt, nor to undergo the hazards of war with them, while these polluted people were forced to send to Jerusalem, and bring their auxiliaries from thence! What friendship, I pray, or what relation was there formerly between them that required this assistance? On the contrary, these people were enemies, and greatly differed from them in their customs. He says, indeed, that they complied immediately, upon their praising them that they should conquer Egypt; as if they did not themselves very well know that country out of which they had been driven by force. Now had these men been in want, or lived miserably, perhaps they might have undertaken so hazardous an enterprise; but as they dwelt in a happy city, and had a large country, and one better than Egypt itself, how came it about that, for the sake of those that had of old been their enemies, of those that were maimed in their bodies, and of those whom none of their own relations would endure, they should run such hazards in assisting them? For they could not foresee that the king would run away from them: on the contrary, he saith himself that "Amenophis's son had three hundred thousand men with him, and met them at Pelusium." Now, to be sure, those that came could not be ignorant of this; but for the king's repentance and flight, how could they possibly guess at it? He then says, that "those who came from Jerusalem, and made this invasion, got the granaries of Egypt into their possession, and perpetrated many of the most horrid actions there." And thence he reproaches them, as though he had not himself introduced them as enemies, or as though he might accuse such as were invited from another place for so doing, when the natural Egyptians themselves had done the same things before their coming, and had taken oaths so to do. However, "Amenophis, some time afterward, came upon them, and conquered them in battle, and slew his enemies, and drove them before him as far as Syria." As if Egypt were so easily taken by people that came from any place whatsoever, and as if those that had conquered it by war, when they were informed that Amenophis was alive, did neither fortify the avenues out of Ethiopia into it, although they had great advantages for doing it, nor did get their other forces ready for their defense! but that he followed them over the sandy desert, and slew them as far as Syria; while yet it is rot an easy thing for an army to pass over that country, even without fighting.

30. Our nation, therefore, according to Manetho, was not derived from Egypt, nor were any of the Egyptians mingled with us. For it is to be supposed that many of the leprous and distempered people were dead in the mines, since they had been there a long time, and in so ill a condition; many others must be dead in the battles that happened afterward, and more still in the last battle and flight after it.

31. It now remains that I debate with Manetho about Moses. Now the Egyptians acknowledge him to have been a wonderful and a divine person; nay, they would willingly lay claim to him themselves, though after a most abusive and incredible manner, and pretend that he was of Heliopolis, and one of the priests of that place, and was ejected out of it among the rest, on account of his leprosy; although it had been demonstrated out of their records that he lived five hundred and eighteen years earlier, and then brought our forefathers out of Egypt into the country that is now inhabited by us. But now that he was not subject in his body to any such calamity, is evident from what he himself tells us; for he forbade those that had the leprosy either to continue in a city, or to inhabit in a village, but commanded that they should go about by themselves with their clothes rent; and declares that such as either touch them, or live under the same roof with them, should be esteemed unclean; nay, more, if any one of their disease be healed, and he recover his natural constitution again, he appointed them certain purifications, and washings with spring water, and the shaving off all their hair, and enjoins that they shall offer many sacrifices, and those of several kinds, and then at length to be admitted into the holy city; although it were to be expected that, on the contrary, if he had been under the same calamity, he should have taken care of such persons beforehand, and have had them treated after a kinder manner, as affected with a concern for those that were to be under the like misfortunes with himself. Nor was it only those leprous people for whose sake he made these laws, but also for such as should be maimed in the smallest part of their body, who yet are not permitted by him to officiate as priests; nay, although any priest, already initiated, should have such a calamity fall upon him afterward, he ordered him to be deprived of his honor of officiating. How can it then be supposed that Moses should ordain such laws against himself, to his own reproach and damage who so ordained them? Nor indeed is that other notion of Manetho at all probable, wherein he relates the change of his name, and says that "he was formerly called Osarsiph;" and this a name no way agreeable to the other, while his true name was Mosses, and signifies a person who is preserved out of the water, for the Egyptians call water Moil. I think, therefore, I have made it sufficiently evident that

Manetho, while he followed his ancient records, did not much mistake the truth of the history; but that when he had recourse to fabulous stories, without any certain author, he either forged them himself, without any probability, or else gave credit to some men who spake so out of their ill-will to us.

32. And now I have done with Manetho, I will inquire into what Cheremon says. For he also, when he pretended to write the Egyptian history, sets down the same name for this king that Manetho did, Amenophis, as also of his son Ramesses, and then goes on thus: "The goddess Isis appeared to Amenophis in his sleep, and blamed him that her temple had been demolished in the war. But that Phritiphantes, the sacred scribe, said to him, that in case he would purge Egypt of the men that had pollutions upon them, he should be no longer troubled with such frightful apparitions. That Amenophis accordingly chose out two hundred and fifty thousand of those that were thus diseased, and cast them out of the country: that Moses and Joseph were scribes, and Joseph was a sacred scribe; that their names were Egyptian originally; that of Moses had been Tisithen, and that of Joseph, Peteseph: that these two came to Pelusium, and lighted upon three hundred and eighty thousand that had been left there by Amenophis, he not being willing to carry them into Egypt; that these scribes made a league of friendship with them, and made with them an expedition against Egypt: that Amenophis could not sustain their attacks, but fled into Ethiopia, and left his wife with child behind him, who lay concealed in certain caverns, and there brought forth a son, whose name was Messene, and who, when he was grown up to man's estate, pursued the Jews into Syria, being about two hundred thousand, and then received his father Amenophis out of Ethiopia."

33. This is the account Cheremon gives us. Now I take it for granted that what I have said already hath plainly proved the falsity of both these narrations; for had there been any real truth at the bottom, it was impossible they should so greatly disagree about the particulars. But for those that invent lies, what they write will easily give us very different accounts, while they forge what they please out of their own heads. Now Manetho says that the king's desire of seeing the gods was the origin of the ejection of the polluted people; but Cheremon feigns that it was a dream of his own, sent upon him by Isis, that was the occasion of it. Manetho says that the person who foreshowed this purgation of Egypt to the king was Amenophis; but this man says it was Phritiphantes. As to the numbers of the multitude that were expelled, they agree exceedingly well [24] the former reckoning them eighty thousand, and the latter about two hundred and fifty thousand! Now, for Manetho, he describes those polluted persons as sent first to work in the quarries, and says that the city Avaris was given them for their habitation. As also

he relates that it was not till after they had made war with the rest of the Egyptians, that they invited the people of Jerusalem to come to their assistance; while Cheremon says only that they were gone out of Egypt, and lighted upon three hundred and eighty thousand men about Pelusium, who had been left there by Amenophis, and so they invaded Egypt with them again; that thereupon Amenophis fled into Ethiopia. But then this Cheremon commits a most ridiculous blunder in not informing us who this army of so many ten thousands were, or whence they came; whether they were native Egyptians, or whether they came from a foreign country. Nor indeed has this man, who forged a dream from Isis about the leprous people, assigned the reason why the king would not bring them into Egypt. Moreover, Cheremon sets down Joseph as driven away at the same time with Moses, who yet died four generations [25] before Moses, which four generations make almost one hundred and seventy years. Besides all this, Ramesses, the son of Amenophis, by Manetho's account, was a young man, and assisted his father in his war, and left the country at the same time with him, and fled into Ethiopia. But Cheremon makes him to have been born in a certain cave, after his father was dead, and that he then overcame the Jews in battle, and drove them into Syria, being in number about two hundred thousand. O the levity of the man! for he had neither told us who these three hundred and eighty thousand were, nor how the four hundred and thirty thousand perished; whether they fell in war, or went over to Ramesses. And, what is the strangest of all, it is not possible to learn out of him who they were whom he calls Jews, or to which of these two parties he applies that denomination, whether to the two hundred and fifty thousand leprous people, or to the three hundred and eighty thousand that were about Pelusium. But perhaps it will be looked upon as a silly thing in me to make any larger confutation of such writers as sufficiently confute themselves; for had they been only confuted by other men, it had been more tolerable.

34. I shall now add to these accounts about Manetho and Cheremon somewhat about Lysimachus, who hath taken the same topic of falsehood with those forementioned, but hath gone far beyond them in the incredible nature of his forgeries; which plainly demonstrates that he contrived them out of his virulent hatred of our nation. His words are these: "The people of the Jews being leprous and scabby, and subject to certain other kinds of distempers, in the days of Bocchoris, king of Egypt, they fled to the temples, and got their food there by begging: and as the numbers were very great that were fallen under these diseases, there arose a scarcity in Egypt. Hereupon Bocehoris, the king of Egypt, sent some to consult the oracle of [Jupiter] Hammon about his scarcity. The god's answer was this, that he must purge his temples of impure and impious men, by expelling

them out of those temples into desert places; but as to the scabby and leprous people, he must drown them, and purge his temples, the sun having an indignation at these men being suffered to live; and by this means the land will bring forth its fruits. Upon Bocchoris's having received these oracles, he called for their priests, and the attendants upon their altars, and ordered them to make a collection of the impure people, and to deliver them to the soldiers, to carry them away into the desert; but to take the leprous people, and wrap them in sheets of lead, and let them down into the sea. Hereupon the scabby and leprous people were drowned, and the rest were gotten together, and sent into desert places, in order to be exposed to destruction. In this case they assembled themselves together, and took counsel what they should do, and determined that, as the night was coming on, they should kindle fires and lamps, and keep watch; that they also should fast the next night, and propitiate the gods, in order to obtain deliverance from them. That on the next day there was one Moses, who advised them that they should venture upon a journey, and go along one road till they should come to places fit for habitation: that he charged them to have no kind regards for any man, nor give good counsel to any, but always to advise them for the worst; and to overturn all those temples and altars of the gods they should meet with: that the rest commended what he had said with one consent, and did what they had resolved on, and so traveled over the desert. But that the difficulties of the journey being over, they came to a country inhabited, and that there they abused the men, and plundered and burnt their temples; and then came into that land which is called Judea, and there they built a city, and dwelt therein, and that their city was named Hierosyla, from this their robbing of the temples; but that still, upon the success they had afterwards, they in time changed its denomination, that it might not be a reproach to them, and called the city Hierosolyma, and themselves Hierosolymites."

35. Now this man did not discover and mention the same king with the others, but feigned a newer name, and passing by the dream and the Egyptian prophet, he brings him to [Jupiter] Hammon, in order to gain oracles about the scabby and leprous people; for he says that the multitude of Jews were gathered together at the temples. Now it is uncertain whether he ascribes this name to these lepers, or to those that were subject to such diseases among the Jews only; for he describes them as a people of the Jews. What people does he mean? foreigners, or those of that country? Why then' dost thou call them Jews, if they were Egyptians? But if they were foreigners, why dost thou not tell us whence they came? And how could it be that, after the king had drowned many of them in the sea, and ejected the rest into desert places, there should be still so great a multitude remaining? Or

after what manner did they pass over the desert, and get the land which we now dwell in, and build our city, and that temple which hath been so famous among all mankind? And besides, he ought to have spoken more about our legislator than by giving us his bare name; and to have informed us of what nation he was, and what parents he was derived from; and to have assigned the reasons why he undertook to make such laws concerning the gods, and concerning matters of injustice with regard to men during that journey. For in case the people were by birth Egyptians, they would not on the sudden have so easily changed the customs of their country; and in case they had been foreigners, they had for certain some laws or other which had been kept by them from long custom. It is true, that with regard to those who had ejected them, they might have sworn never to bear good-will to them, and might have had a plausible reason for so doing. But if these men resolved to wage an implacable war against all men, in case they had acted as wickedly as he relates of them, and this while they wanted the assistance of all men, this demonstrates a kind of mad conduct indeed; but not of the men themselves, but very greatly so of him that tells such lies about them. He hath also impudence enough to say that a name, implying "Robbers of the temples,"[26] was given to their city, and that this name was afterward changed. The reason of which is plain, that the former name brought reproach and hatred upon them in the times of their posterity, while, it seems, those that built the city thought they did honor to the city by giving it such a name. So we see that this fine fellow had such an unbounded inclination to reproach us, that he did not understand that robbery of temples is not expressed By the same word and name among the Jews as it is among the Greeks. But why should a man say any more to a person who tells such impudent lies? However, since this book is arisen to a competent length, I will make another beginning, and endeavor to add what still remains to perfect my design in the following book

APION BOOK I: FOOTNOTES

[1] This first book has a wrong title. It is not written against Apion, as is the first part of the second book, but against those Greeks in general who would not believe Josephus's former accounts of the very ancient state of the Jewish nation, in his 20 books of Antiquities; and particularly against Agatharelddes, Manetho, Cheremon, and Lysimachus. it is one of the most learned, excellent, and useful books of all antiquity; and upon Jerome's perusal of this and the following book, he declares that it seems to him a miraculous thing "how one that was a Hebrew, who had been from his infancy instructed in sacred learning, should be able to pronounce such a number of testimonies out of profane authors, as if he had read

over all the Grecian libraries," Epist. 8. ad Magnum; and the learned Jew, Manasseh-Ben-Israel, esteemed these two books so excellent, as to translate them into the Hebrew; this we learn from his own catalogue of his works, which I have seen. As to the time and place when and where these two books were written, the learned have not hitherto been able to determine them any further than that they were written some time after his Antiquities, or some time after A.D. 93; which indeed is too obvious at their entrance to be overlooked by even a careless peruser, they being directly intended against those that would not believe what he had advanced in those books con-the great of the Jewish nation As to the place, they all imagine that these two books were written where the former were, I mean at Rome; and I confess that I myself believed both those determinations, till I came to finish my notes upon these books, when I met with plain indications that they were written not at Rome, but in Judea, and this after the third of Trajan, or A.D. 100.

[2] Take Dr. Hudson's note here, which as it justly contradicts the common opinion that Josephus either died under Domitian, or at least wrote nothing later than his days, so does it perfectly agree to my own determination, from Justus of Tiberias, that he wrote or finished his own Life after the third of Trajan, or A.D. 100. To which Noldius also agrees, de Herod, No. 383 [Epaphroditus]. "Since Florius Josephus," says Dr. Hudson, "wrote [or finished] his books of Antiquities on the thirteenth of Domitian, [A.D. 93,] and after that wrote the Memoirs of his own Life, as an appendix to the books of Antiquities, and at last his two books against Apion, and yet dedicated all those writings to Epaphroditus; he can hardly be that Epaphroditus who was formerly secretary to Nero, and was slain on the fourteenth [or fifteenth] of Domitian, after he had been for a good while in banishment; but another Epaphroditas, a freed-man, and procurator of Trajan, as says Grotius on Luke 1:3."

[3] The preservation of Homer's Poems by memory, and not by his own writing them down, and that thence they were styled Rhapsodies, as sung by him, like ballads, by parts, and not composed and connected together in complete works, are opinions well known from the ancient commentators; though such supposal seems to myself, as well as to Fabricius Biblioth. Grace. I. p. 269, and to others, highly improbable. Nor does Josephus say there were no ancienter writings among the Greeks than Homer's Poems, but that they did not fully own any ancienter writings pretending to such antiquity, which is trite.

[4] It well deserves to be considered, that Josephus here says how all the following Greek historians looked on Herodotus as a fabulous author; and presently, sect. 14, how Manetho, the most authentic writer of the Egyptian

history, greatly complains of his mistakes in the Egyptian affairs; as also that Strabo, B. XI. p. 507, the most accurate geographer and historian, esteemed him such; that Xenophon, the much more accurate historian in the affairs of Cyrus, implies that Herodotus's account of that great man is almost entirely romantic. See the notes on Antiq. B. XI. ch. 2. sect. 1, and Hutchinson's Prolegomena to his edition of Xenophon's, that we have already seen in the note on Antiq. B. VIII. ch. 10. sect. 3, how very little Herodotus knew about the Jewish affairs and country, and that he greatly affected what we call the marvelous, as Monsieur Rollin has lately and justly determined; whence we are not always to depend on the authority of Herodotus, where it is unsupported by other evidence, but ought to compare the other evidence with his, and if it preponderate, to prefer it before his. I do not mean by this that Herodotus willfully related what he believed to be false, [as Cteeias seems to have done,] but that he often wanted evidence, and sometimes preferred what was marvelous to what was best attested as really true.

⁵ About the days of Cyrus and Daniel.

⁶ It is here well worth our observation, what the reasons are that such ancient authors as Herodotus, Josephus, and others have been read to so little purpose by many learned critics; viz. that their main aim has not been chronology or history, but philology, to know words, and not things, they not much entering oftentimes into the real contents of their authors, and judging which were the most accurate discoverers of truth, and most to be depended on in the several histories, but rather inquiring who wrote the finest style, and had the greatest elegance in their expressions; which are things of small consequence in comparison of the other. Thus you will sometimes find great debates among the learned, whether Herodotus or Thucydides were the finest historian in the Ionic and Attic ways of writing; which signify little as to the real value of each of their histories; while it would be of much more moment to let the reader know, that as the consequence of Herodotus's history, which begins so much earlier, and reaches so much wider, than that of Thucydides, is therefore vastly greater; so is the most part of Thucydides, which belongs to his own times, and fell under his own observation, much the most certain.

⁷ Of this accuracy of the Jews before and in our Savior's time, in carefully preserving their genealogies all along, particularly those of the priests, see Josephus's Life, sect. 1. This accuracy. seems to have ended at the destruction of Jerusalem by Titus, or, however, at that by Adrian.

⁸ Which were these twenty-two sacred books of the Old Testament, see the Supplement to the Essay of the Old Testament, p. 25-29, viz. those we call canonical, all excepting the Canticles; but still with this further exception, that the

book of apocryphal Esdras be taken into that number instead of our canonical Ezra, which seems to be no more than a later epitome of the other; which two books of Canticles and Ezra it no way appears that our Josephus ever saw.

[9] Here we have an account of the first building of the city of Jerusalem, according to Manetho, when the Phoenician shepherds were expelled out of Egypt about thirty-seven years before Abraham came out of Harsh.

[10] Genesis 46;32, 34; 47:3, 4.

[11] In our copies of the book of Genesis and of Joseph, this Joseph never calls himself "a captive," when he was with the king of Egypt, though he does call himself "a servant," "a slave," or "captive," many times in the Testament of the Twelve Patriarchs, under Joseph, sect. 1, 11, 13-16.

[12] Of this Egyptian chronology of Manetho, as mistaken by Josephus, and of these Phoenician shepherds, as falsely supposed by him, and others after him, to have been the Israelites in Egypt, see Essay on the Old Testament, Appendix, p. 182-188. And note here, that when Josephus tells us that the Greeks or Argives looked on this Danaus as "a most ancient," or "the most ancient," king of Argos, he need not be supposed to mean, in the strictest sense, that they had no one king so ancient as he; for it is certain that they owned nine kings before him, and Inachus at the head of them. See Authentic Records, Part II. p. 983, as Josephus could not but know very well; but that he was esteemed as very ancient by them, and that they knew they had been first of all denominated "Danai" from this very ancient king Danaus. Nor does this superlative degree always imply the "most ancient" of all without exception, but is sometimes to be rendered "very ancient" only, as is the case in the like superlative degrees of other words also.

[13] Authentic Records, Part II. p. 983, as Josephus could not but know very well; but that he was esteemed as very ancient by them, and that they knew they had been first of all denominated "Danai" from this very ancient king Danaus. Nor does this superlative degree always imply the "most ancient" of all without exception, but is sometimes to be rendered "very ancient" only, as is the case in the like superlative degrees of other words also.

[14] This number in Josephus, that Nebuchadnezzar destroyed the temple in the eighteenth year of his reign, is a mistake in the nicety of chronology; for it was in the nineteenth. The true number here for the year of Darius, in which the second temple was finished, whether the second with our present copies, or the sixth with that of Syncellus, or the tenth with that of Eusebius, is very uncertain; so we had best follow Josephus's own account elsewhere, Antiq.;B. XI. ch. 3. sect. 4, which shows us that according to his copy of the Old Testament, after the second of Cyrus, that work was interrupted till the second of Darius, when in seven years it

was finished in the ninth of Darius.

[15] This is a thing well known by the learned, that we are not secure that we have any genuine writings of Pythagoras; those Golden Verses, which are his best remains, being generally supposed to have been written not by himself, but by some of his scholars only, in agreement with what Josephus here affirms of him.]

[16] Whether these verses of Cherilus, the heathen poet, in the days of Xerxes, belong to the Solymi in Pisidia, that were near a small lake, or to the Jews that dwelt on the Solymean or Jerusalem mountains, near the great and broad lake Asphaltitis, that were a strange people, and spake the Phoenician tongue, is not agreed on by the learned. If is yet certain that Josephus here, and Eusebius, Prep. IX. 9. p. 412, took them to be Jews; and I confess I cannot but very much incline to the same opinion. The other Solymi were not a strange people, but heathen idolaters, like the other parts of Xerxes's army; and that these spake the Phoenician tongue is next to impossible, as the Jews certainly did; nor is there the least evidence for it elsewhere. Nor was the lake adjoining to the mountains of the Solvmi at all large or broad, in comparison of the Jewish lake Asphaltitis; nor indeed were these so considerable a people as the Jews, nor so likely to be desired by Xerxes for his army as the Jews, to whom he was always very favorable. As for the rest of Cherilus's description, that "their heads were sooty; that they had round rasures on their heads; that their heads and faces were like nasty horse-heads, which had been hardened in the smoke;" these awkward characters probably fitted the Solymi of Pisidi no better than they did the Jews in Judea. And indeed this reproachful language, here given these people, is to me a strong indication that they were the poor despicable Jews, and not the Pisidian Solymi celebrated in Homer, whom Cherilus here describes; nor are we to expect that either Cherilus or Hecateus, or any other pagan writers cited by Josephus and Eusebius, made no mistakes in the Jewish history. If by comparing their testimonies with the more authentic records of that nation we find them for the main to confirm the same, as we almost always do, we ought to be satisfied, and not expect that they ever had an exact knowledge of all the circumstances of the Jewish affairs, which indeed it was almost always impossible for them to have. See sect. 23.

[17] This Hezekiah, who is here called a high priest, is not named in Josephus's catalogue; the real high priest at that time being rather Onias, as Archbishop Usher supposes. However, Josephus often uses the word high priests in the plural number, as living many at the same time. See the note on Antiq. B. XX. ch. 8. sect. 8.

[18] So I read the text with Havercamp, though the place be difficult.

[19] This number of arourae or Egyptian acres, 3,000,000, each aroura containing a square of 100 Egyptian cubits, [being about three quarters of an English acre, and just twice the area of the court of the Jewish tabernacle,] as contained in the country of Judea, will be about one third of the entire number of arourae in the whole land of Judea, supposing it 160 measured miles long and 70 such miles broad; which estimation, for the fruitful parts of it, as perhaps here in Hecateus, is not therefore very wide from the truth. The fifty furlongs in compass for the city Jerusalem presently are not very wide from the truth also, as Josephus himself describes it, who, Of the War, B. V. ch. 4. sect. 3. makes its wall thirty-three furlongs, besides the suburbs and gardens; nay, he says, B. V. ch. 12. sect. 2, that Titus's wall about it at some small distance, after the gardens and suburbs were destroyed, was not less than thirty-nine furlongs. Nor perhaps were its constant inhabitants, in the days of Hecateus, many more than these 120,000, because room was always to be left for vastly greater numbers which came up at the three great festivals; to say nothing of the probable increase in their number between the days of Hecateus and Josephus, which was at least three hundred years. But see a more authentic account of some of these measures in my Description of the Jewish Temples. However, we are not to expect that such heathens as Cherilus or Hecateus, or the rest that are cited by Josephus and Eusebius, could avoid making many mistakes in the Jewish history, while yet they strongly confirm the same history in the general, and are most valuable attestations to those more authentic accounts we have in the Scriptures and Josephus concerning them.

[20] A glorious testimony this of the observation of the sabbath by the Jews. See Antiq. B. XVI. ch. 2. sect. 4, and ch. 6. sect. 2; the Life, sect. 54; and War, B. IV. ch. 9. sect. 12.

[21] Not their law, but the superstitious interpretation of their leaders which neither the Maccabees nor our blessed Savior did ever approve of.

[22] In reading this and the remaining sections of this book, and some parts of the next, one may easily perceive that our usually cool and candid author, Josephus, was too highly offended with the impudent calumnies of Manethe, and the other bitter enemies of the Jews, with whom he had now to deal, and was thereby betrayed into a greater heat and passion than ordinary, and that by consequence he does not hear reason with his usual fairness and impartiality; he seems to depart sometimes from the brevity and sincerity of a faithful historian, which is his grand character, and indulges the prolixity and colors of a pleader and a disputant: accordingly, I confess, I always read these sections with less pleasure than I do the rest of his writings, though I fully believe the reproaches cast on the

Jews, which he here endeavors to confute and expose, were wholly groundless and unreasonable.

[23] This is a very valuable testimony of Manetho, that the laws of Osarsiph, or Moses, were not made in compliance with, but in opposition to, the customs of the Egyptians. See the note on Antiq. B. III. ch. 8. sect. 9.

[24] By way of irony, I suppose.

[25] Here we see that Josephus esteemed a generation between Joseph and Moses to be about forty-two or forty-three years; which, if taken between the earlier children, well agrees with the duration of human life in those ages. See Antheat. Rec. Part II. pages 966, 1019, 1020.

[26] That is the meaning of Hierosyla in Greek, not in Hebrew.

BOOK II

1. In the former book, most honored Epaphroditus, I have demonstrated our antiquity, and confirmed the truth of what I have said, from the writings of the Phoenicians, and Chaldeans, and Egyptians. I have, moreover, produced many of the Grecian writers as witnesses thereto. I have also made a refutation of Manetho and Cheremon, and of certain others of our enemies. I shall now [1] therefore begin a confutation of the remaining authors who have written any thing against us; although I confess I have had a doubt upon me about Apion [2] the grammarian, whether I ought to take the trouble of confuting him or not; for some of his writings contain much the same accusations which the others have laid against us, some things that he hath added are very frigid and contemptible, and for the greatest part of what he says, it is very scurrilous, and, to speak no more than the plain truth, it shows him to be a very unlearned person, and what he lays together looks like the work of a man of very bad morals, and of one no better in his whole life than a mountebank. Yet, because there are a great many men so very foolish, that they are rather caught by such orations than by what is written with care, and take pleasure in reproaching other men, and cannot abide to hear them commended, I thought it to be necessary not to let this man go off without examination, who had written such an accusation against us, as if he would bring us to make an answer in open court. For I also have observed, that many men are very much delighted when they see a man who first began to reproach another, to be himself exposed to contempt on account of the vices he hath himself been guilty of. However, it is not a very easy thing to go over this man's discourse, nor to know plainly what he means; yet does he seem, amidst a great confusion and disorder in his falsehoods, to produce, in the first place, such things as resemble what we have examined already, and relate to the departure of our forefathers out of Egypt; and, in the second place, he accuses those Jews that are inhabitants of Alexandria; as, in the third place, he mixes with those things such accusations as concern the sacred purifications, with the other legal rites used in the temple.

2. Now although I cannot but think that I have already demonstrated, and that abundantly more than was necessary, that our fathers were not originally Egyptians, nor were thence expelled, either on account of bodily diseases, or any other calamities of that sort; yet will I briefly take notice of what Apion adds upon that subject; for in his third book, which relates to the affairs of Egypt, he speaks

thus: "I have heard of the ancient men of Egypt, that Moses was of Heliopolis, and that he thought himself obliged to follow the customs of his forefathers, and offered his prayers in the open air, towards the city walls; but that he reduced them all to be directed towards sun-rising, which was agreeable to the situation of Heliopolis; that he also set up pillars instead of gnomons, [3] under which was represented a cavity like that of a boat, and the shadow that fell from their tops fell down upon that cavity, that it might go round about the like course as the sun itself goes round in the other." This is that wonderful relation which we have given us by this grammarian. But that it is a false one is so plain, that it stands in need of few words to prove it, but is manifest from the works of Moses; for when he erected the first tabernacle to God, he did himself neither give order for any such kind of representation to be made at it, nor ordain that those that came after him should make such a one. Moreover, when in a future age Solomon built his temple in Jerusalem, he avoided all such needless decorations as Apion hath here devised. He says further, how he had "heard of the ancient men, that Moses was of Hellopolis." To be sure that was, because being a younger man himself, he believed those that by their elder age were acquainted and conversed with him. Now this grammarian, as he was, could not certainly tell which was the poet Homer's country, no more than he could which was the country of Pythagoras, who lived comparatively but a little while ago; yet does he thus easily determine the age of Moses, who preceded them such a vast number of years, as depending on his ancient men's relation, which shows how notorious a liar he was. But then as to this chronological determination of the time when he says he brought the leprous people, the blind, and the lame out of Egypt, see how well this most accurate grammarian of ours agrees with those that have written before him! Manetho says that the Jews departed out of Egypt, in the reign of Tethmosis, three hundred ninety-three years before Danaus fled to Argos; Lysimaehus says it was under king Bocchoris, that is, one thousand seven hundred years ago; Molo and some others determined it as every one pleased: but this Apion of ours, as deserving to be believed before them, hath determined it exactly to have been in the seventh olympiad, and the first year of that olympiad; the very same year in which he says that Carthage was built by the Phoenicians. The reason why he added this building of Carthage was, to be sure, in order, as he thought, to strengthen his assertion by so evident a character of chronology. But he was not aware that this character confutes his assertion; for if we may give credit to the Phoenician records as to the time of the first coming of their colony to Carthage, they relate that Hirom their king was above a hundred and fifty years earlier than the building of Carthage; concerning whom I have formerly produced testimonials out of those Phoenician records, as also that this Hirom was a friend of Solomon when he was building the temple of Jerusalem, and gave him great assistance in his building that temple; while still Solomon himself built that temple six hundred and twelve years after the Jews came out of Egypt. As for the number of those that were expelled out of Egypt, he hath contrived to have the very same number with Lysimaehus, and says they were a hundred and ten thousand. He then assigns a certain wonderful and plausible occasion for the name of Sabbath; for he says that "when the Jews had traveled a six days' journey, they had buboes in their groins; and that on this account it was that they rested on the seventh day, as having got safely to that country which is now called Judea; that then they preserved the language of the Egyptians, and called that day the Sabbath, for that malady of buboes on their groin was named Sabbatosis by the Egyptians." And would not a man now laugh at this fellow's trifling, or rather hate his impudence in writing thus? We must, it seems, take it for granted that all these hundred and ten thousand men must have these buboes. But, for certain, if those men had been blind and lame, and had all sorts of distempers upon them, as Apion says they had, they could not have gone one single day's journey; but if they had been all able to travel over a large desert, and, besides that, to fight and conquer those that opposed them, they had not all of them had buboes on their groins after the sixth day was over; for no such distemper comes naturally and of necessity upon those that travel; but still, when there are many ten thousands in a camp together, they constantly march a settled space [in a day]. Nor is it at all probable that such a thing should happen by chance; this would be prodigiously absurd to be supposed. However, our admirable author Apion hath before told us that "they came to Judea in six days' time;" and again, that "Moses went up to a mountain that lay between Egypt and Arabia, which was called Sinai, and was concealed there forty days, and that when he came down from thence he gave laws to the Jews." But, then, how was it possible for them to tarry forty days in a desert place where there was no water, and at the same time to pass all over the country between that and Judea in the six days? And as for this grammatical translation of the word Sabbath, it either contains an instance of his great impudence or gross ignorance; for the words Sabbo and Sabbath are widely different from one another; for the word Sabbath in the Jewish language denotes rest from all sorts of work; but the word Sabbo, as he affirms, denotes among the Egyptians the malady of a bubo in the groin.

    3. This is that novel account which the Egyptian Apion gives us concerning the Jews' departure out of Egypt, and is no better than a contrivance of his own. But why should we wonder at the lies he tells about our forefathers, when he

affirms them to be of Egyptian original, when he lies also about himself? for although he was born at Oasis in Egypt, he pretends to be, as a man may say, the top man of all the Egyptians; yet does he forswear his real country and progenitors, and by falsely pretending to be born at Alexandria, cannot deny the [4] pravity of his family; for you see how justly he calls those Egyptians whom he hates, and endeavors to reproach; for had he not deemed Egyptians to be a name of great reproach, he would not have avoided the name of an Egyptian himself; as we know that those who brag of their own countries value themselves upon the denomination they acquire thereby, and reprove such as unjustly lay claim thereto. As for the Egyptians' claim to be of our kindred, they do it on one of the following accounts; I mean, either as they value themselves upon it, and pretend to bear that relation to us; or else as they would draw us in to be partakers of their own infamy. But this fine fellow Apion seems to broach this reproachful appellation against us, [that we were originally Egyptians,] in order to bestow it on the Alexandrians, as a reward for the privilege they had given him of being a fellow citizen with them: he also is apprized of the ill-will the Alexandrians bear to those Jews who are their fellow citizens, and so proposes to himself to reproach them, although he must thereby include all the other Egyptians also; while in both cases he is no better than an impudent liar.

4. But let us now see what those heavy and wicked crimes are which Apion charges upon the Alexandrian Jews. "They came [says he] out of Syria, and inhabited near the tempestuous sea, and were in the neighborhood of the dashing of the waves." Now if the place of habitation includes any thing that is reproached, this man reproaches not his own real country, [Egypt,] but what he pretends to be his own country, Alexandria; for all are agreed in this, that the part of that city which is near the sea is the best part of all for habitation. Now if the Jews gained that part of the city by force, and have kept it hitherto without impeachment, this is a mark of their valor; but in reality it was Alexander himself that gave them that place for their habitation, when they obtained equal privileges there with the Macedonians. Nor call I devise what Apion would have said, had their habitation been at Necropolis? and not been fixed hard by the royal palace [as it is]; nor had their nation had the denomination of Macedonians given them till this very day [as they have]. Had this man now read the epistles of king Alexander, or those of Ptolemy the son of Lagus, or met with the writings of the succeeding kings, or that pillar which is still standing at Alexandria, and contains the privileges which the great [Julius] Caesar bestowed upon the Jews; had this man, I say, known these records, and yet hath the impudence to write in contradiction to them, he hath shown himself to be a wicked man; but if he knew

nothing of these records, he hath shown himself to be a man very ignorant: nay, when lie appears to wonder how Jews could be called Alexandrians, this is another like instance of his ignorance; for all such as are called out to be colonies, although they be ever so far remote from one another in their original, receive their names from those that bring them to their new habitations. And what occasion is there to speak of others, when those of us Jews that dwell at Antioch are named Antiochians, because Seleucns the founder of that city gave them the privileges belonging thereto? After the like manner do those Jews that inhabit Ephesus, and the other cities of Ionia, enjoy the same name with those that were originally born there, by the grant of the succeeding princes; nay, the kindness and humanity of the Romans hath been so great, that it hath granted leave to almost all others to take the same name of Romans upon them; I mean not particular men only, but entire and large nations themselves also; for those anciently named Iberi, and Tyrrheni, and Sabini, are now called Romani. And if Apion reject this way of obtaining the privilege of a citizen of Alexandria, let him abstain from calling himself an Alexandrian hereafter; for otherwise, how can he who was born in the very heart of Egypt be an Alexandrian, if this way of accepting such a privilege, of which he would have us deprived, be once abrogated? although indeed these Romans, who are now the lords of the habitable earth, have forbidden the Egyptians to have the privileges of any city whatsoever; while this fine fellow, who is willing to partake of such a privilege himself as he is forbidden to make use of, endeavors by calumnies to deprive those of it that have justly received it; for Alexander did not therefore get some of our nation to Alexandria, because he wanted inhabitants for this his city, on whose building he had bestowed so much pains; but this was given to our people as a reward, because he had, upon a careful trial, found them all to have been men of virtue and fidelity to him; for, as Hecateus says concerning us, "Alexander honored our nation to such a degree, that, for the equity and the fidelity which the Jews exhibited to him, he permitted them to hold the country of Samaria free from tribute. Of the same mind also was Ptolemy the son of Lagus, as to those Jews who dwelt at Alexandria." For he intrusted the fortresses of Egypt into their hands, as believing they would keep them faithfully and valiantly for him; and when he was desirous to secure the government of Cyrene, and the other cities of Libya, to himself, he sent a party of Jews to inhabit in them. And for his successor Ptolemy, who was called Philadelphus, he did not only set all those of our nation free who were captives under him, but did frequently give money [for their ransom]; and, what was his greatest work of all, he had a great desire of knowing our laws, and of obtaining the books of our sacred Scriptures; accordingly, he desired that such men might be sent him as might interpret our law to him; and, in order to have them well compiled, he committed that care to no ordinary persons, but ordained that Demetrius Phalereus, and Andreas, and Aristeas; the first, Demetrius, the most learned person of his age, and the others, such as were intrusted with the guard of his body; should take care of this matter: nor would he certainly have been so desirous of learning our law, and the philosophy of our nation, had he despised the men that made use of it, or had he not indeed had them in great admiration.

5. Now this Apion was unacquainted with almost all the kings of those Macedonians whom he pretends to have been his progenitors, who were yet very well affected towards us; for the third of those Ptolemies, who was called Euergetes, when he had gotten possession of all Syria by force, did not offer his thank-offerings to the Egyptian gods for his victory, but came to Jerusalem, and according to our own laws offered many sacrifices to God, and dedicated to him such gifts as were suitable to such a victory: and as for Ptolemy Philometer and his wife Cleopatra, they committed their whole kingdom to the Jews, when Onias and Dositheus, both Jews, whose names are laughed at by Apion, were the generals of their whole army. But certainly, instead of reproaching them, he ought to admire their actions, and return them thanks for saving Alexandria, whose citizen he pretends to be; for when these Alexandrians were making war with Cleopatra the queen, and were in danger of being utterly ruined, these Jews brought them to terms of agreement, and freed them from the miseries of a civil war. "But then [says Apion] Onias brought a small army afterward upon the city at the time when Thorruns the Roman ambassador was there present." Yes, do I venture to say, and that he did rightly and very justly in so doing; for that Ptolemy who was called Physco, upon the death of his brother Philometer, came from Cyrene, and would have ejected Cleopatra as well as her sons out of their kingdom, that he might obtain it for himself unjustly.[5] For this cause then it was that Onias undertook a war against him on Cleopatra's account; nor would he desert that trust the royal family had reposed in him in their distress. Accordingly, God gave a remarkable attestation to his righteous procedure; for when Ptolemy Physco [6] had the presumption to fight against Onias's army, and had caught all the Jews that were in the city [Alexandria], with their children and wives, and exposed them naked and in bonds to his elephants, that they might be trodden upon and destroyed, and when he had made those elephants drunk for that purpose, the event proved contrary to his preparations; for these elephants left the Jews who were exposed to them, and fell violently upon Physco's friends, and slew a great number of them; nay, after this Ptolemy saw a terrible ghost, which prohibited his hurting those men; his very concubine, whom he loved so well, [some call her Ithaca, and

others Irene,] making supplication to him, that he would not perpetrate so great a wickedness. So he complied with her request, and repented of what he either had already done, or was about to do; whence it is well known that the Alexandrian Jews do with good reason celebrate this day, on the account that they had thereon been vouchsafed such an evident deliverance from God. However, Apion, the common calumniator of men, hath the presumption to accuse the Jews for making this war against Physco, when he ought to have commended them for the same. This man also makes mention of Cleopatra, the last queen of Alexandria, and abuses us, because she was ungrateful to us; whereas he ought to have reproved her, who indulged herself in all kinds of injustice and wicked practices, both with regard to her nearest relations and husbands who had loved her, and, indeed, in general with regard to all the Romans, and those emperors that were her benefactors; who also had her sister Arsinoe slain in a temple, when she had done her no harm: moreover, she had her brother slain by private treachery, and she destroyed the gods of her country and the sepulchers of her progenitors; and while she had received her kingdom from the first Caesar, she had the impudence to rebel against his son:[7] and successor; nay, she corrupted Antony with her love-tricks, and rendered him an enemy to his country, and made him treacherous to his friends, and [by his means] despoiled some of their royal authority, and forced others in her madness to act wickedly. But what need I enlarge upon this head any further, when she left Antony in his fight at sea, though he were her husband, and the father of their common children, and compelled him to resign up his government, with the army, and to follow her [into Egypt]? nay, when last of all Caesar had taken Alexandria, she came to that pitch of cruelty, that she declared she had some hope of preserving her affairs still, in case she could kill the Jews, though it were with her own hand; to such a degree of barbarity and perfidiousness had she arrived. And doth any one think that we cannot boast ourselves of any thing, if, as Apion says, this queen did not at a time of famine distribute wheat among us? However, she at length met with the punishment she deserved. As for us Jews, we appeal to the great Caesar what assistance we brought him, and what fidelity we showed to him against the Egyptians; as also to the senate and its decrees, and the epistles of Augustus Caesar, whereby our merits [to the Romans] are justified. Apion ought to have looked upon those epistles, and in particular to have examined the testimonies given on our behalf, under Alexander and all the Ptolemies, and the decrees of the senate and of the greatest Roman emperors. And if Germanicus was not able to make a distribution of corn to all the inhabitants of Alexandria, that only shows what a barren time it was, and how great a want there was then of corn, but tends nothing to the accusation of the Jews; for what all the emperors have thought of the Alexandrian Jews is well known, for this distribution of wheat was no otherwise omitted with regard to the Jews, than it was with regard to the other inhabitants of Alexandria. But they still were desirous to preserve what the kings had formerly intrusted to their care, I mean the custody of the river; nor did those kings think them unworthy of having the entire custody thereof, upon all occasions.

6. But besides this, Apion objects to us thus: "If the Jews [says he] be citizens of Alexandria, why do they not worship the same gods with the Alexandrians?" To which I give this answer: Since you are yourselves Egyptians, why do you fight it out one against another, and have implacable wars about your religion? At this rate we must not call you all Egyptians, nor indeed in general men, because you breed up with great care beasts of a nature quite contrary to that of men, although the nature of all men seems to be one and the same. Now if there be such differences in opinion among you Egyptians, why are you surprised that those who came to Alexandria from another country, and had original laws of their own before, should persevere in the observance of those laws? But still he charges us with being the authors of sedition; which accusation, if it be a just one, why is it not laid against us all, since we are known to be all of one mind. Moreover, those that search into such matters will soon discover that the authors of sedition have been such citizens of Alexandria as Apion is; for while they were the Grecians and Macedonians who were ill possession of this city, there was no sedition raised against us, and we were permitted to observe our ancient solemnities; but when the number of the Egyptians therein came to be considerable, the times grew confused, and then these seditions brake out still more and more, while our people continued uncorrupted. These Egyptians, therefore, were the authors of these troubles, who having not the constancy of Macedonians, nor the prudence of Grecians, indulged all of them the evil manners of the Egyptians, and continued their ancient hatred against us; for what is here so presumptuously charged upon us, is owing to the differences that are amongst themselves; while many of them have not obtained the privileges of citizens in proper times, but style those who are well known to have had that privilege extended to them all no other than foreigners: for it does not appear that any of the kings have ever formerly bestowed those privileges of citizens upon Egyptians, no more than have the emperors done it more lately; while it was Alexander who introduced us into this city at first, the kings augmented our privileges therein, and the Romans have been pleased to preserve them always inviolable. Moreover, Apion would lay a blot upon us, because we do not erect images for our emperors; as if those emperors

did not know this before, or stood in need of Apion as their defender; whereas he ought rather to have admired the magnanimity and modesty of the Romans, whereby they do not compel those that are subject to them to transgress the laws of their countries, but are willing to receive the honors due to them after such a manner as those who are to pay them esteem consistent with piety and with their own laws; for they do not thank people for conferring honors upon them, When they are compelled by violence so to do. Accordingly, since the Grecians and some other nations think it a right thing to make images, nay, when they have painted the pictures of their parents, and wives, and children, they exult for joy; and some there are who take pictures for themselves of such persons as were no way related to them; nay, some take the pictures of such servants as they were fond of; what wonder is it then if such as these appear willing to pay the same respect to their princes and lords? But then our legislator hath forbidden us to make images, not by way of denunciation beforehand, that the Roman authority was not to be honored, but as despising a thing that was neither necessary nor useful for either God or man; and he forbade them, as we shall prove hereafter, to make these images for any part of the animal creation, and much less for God himself, who is no part of such animal creation. Yet hath our legislator no where forbidden us to pay honors to worthy men, provided they be of another kind, and inferior to those we pay to God; with which honors we willingly testify our respect to our emperors, and to the people of Rome; we also offer perpetual sacrifices for them; nor do we only offer them every day at the common expenses of all the Jews, but although we offer no other such sacrifices out of our common expenses, no, not for our own children, yet do we this as a peculiar honor to the emperors, and to them alone, while we do the same to no other person whomsoever. And let this suffice for an answer in general to Apion, as to what he says with relation to the Alexandrian Jews.

7. However, I cannot but admire those other authors who furnished this man with such his materials; I mean Possidonius and Apollonius [the son of] Molo,[8] who, while they accuse us for not worshipping the same gods whom others worship, they think themselves not guilty of impiety when they tell lies of us, and frame absurd and reproachful stories about our temple; whereas it is a most shameful thing for freemen to forge lies on any occasion, and much more so to forge them about our temple, which was so famous over all the world, and was preserved so sacred by us; for Apion hath the impudence to pretend that, "the Jews placed an ass's head in their holy place;" and he affirms that this was discovered when Antiochus Epiphanes spoiled our temple, and found that ass's head there made of gold, and worth a great deal of money. To this my first answer

shall be this, that had there been any such thing among us, an Egyptian ought by no means to have thrown it in our teeth, since an ass is not a more contemptible animal than [9] and goats, and other such creatures, which among them are gods. But besides this answer, I say further, how comes it about that Apion does not understand this to be no other than a palpable lie, and to be confuted by the thing itself as utterly incredible? For we Jews are always governed by the same laws, in which we constantly persevere; and although many misfortunes have befallen our city, as the like have befallen others, and although Theos [Epiphanes], and Pompey the Great, and Licinius Crassus, and last of all Titus Caesar, have conquered us in war, and gotten possession of our temple; yet have they none of them found any such thing there, nor indeed any thing but what was agreeable to the strictest piety; although what they found we are not at liberty to reveal to other nations. But for Antiochus [Epiphanes], he had no just cause for that ravage in our temple that he made; he only came to it when he wanted money, without declaring himself our enemy, and attacked us while we were his associates and his friends; nor did he find any thing there that was ridiculous. This is attested by many worthy writers; Polybius of Megalopolis, Strabo of Cappadocia, Nicolaus of Damascus, Timagenes, Castor the chronotoger, and Apollodorus; [10] who all say that it was out of Antiochus's want of money that he broke his league with the Jews, and despoiled their temple when it was full of gold and silver. Apion ought to have had a regard to these facts, unless he had himself had either an ass's heart or a dog's impudence; of such a dog I mean as they worship; for he had no other external reason for the lies he tells of us. As for us Jews, we ascribe no honor or power to asses, as do the Egyptians to crocodiles and asps, when they esteem such as are seized upon by the former, or bitten by the latter, to be happy persons, and persons worthy of God. Asses are the same with us which they are with other wise men, viz. creatures that bear the burdens that we lay upon them; but if they come to our thrashing-floors and eat our corn, or do not perform what we impose upon them, we beat them with a great many stripes, because it is their business to minister to us in our husbandry affairs. But this Apion of ours was either perfectly unskillful in the composition of such fallacious discourses, or however, when he begun [somewhat better], he was not able to persevere in what he had undertaken, since he hath no manner of success in those reproaches he casts upon us.

8. He adds another Grecian fable, in order to reproach us. In reply to which, it would be enough to say, that they who presume to speak about Divine worship ought not to be ignorant of this plain truth, that it is a degree of less impurity to pass through temples, than to forge wicked calumnies of its priests. Now such men as he are more zealous to justify a sacrilegious king, than to write what is just and

what is true about us, and about our temple; for when they are desirous of gratifying Antiochus, and of concealing that perfidiousness and sacrilege which he was guilty of, with regard to our nation, when he wanted money, they endeavor to disgrace us, and tell lies even relating to futurities. Apion becomes other men's prophet upon this occasion, and says that "Antiochus found in our temple a bed, and a man lying upon it, with a small table before him, full of dainties, from the [fishes of the] sea, and the fowls of the dry land; that this man was amazed at these dainties thus set before him; that he immediately adored the king, upon his coming in, as hoping that he would afford him all possible assistance; that he fell down upon his knees, and stretched out to him his right hand, and begged to be released; and that when the king bid him sit down, and tell him who he was, and why he dwelt there, and what was the meaning of those various sorts of food that were set before him the man made a lamentable complaint, and with sighs, and tears in his eyes, gave him this account of the distress he was in; and said that he was a Greek and that as he went over this province, in order to get his living, he was seized upon by foreigners, on a sudden, and brought to this temple, and shut up therein, and was seen by nobody, but was fattened by these curious provisions thus set before him; and that truly at the first such unexpected advantages seemed to him matter of great joy; that after a while, they brought a suspicion him, and at length astonishment, what their meaning should be; that at last he inquired of the servants that came to him and was by them informed that it was in order to the fulfilling a law of the Jews, which they must not tell him, that he was thus fed; and that they did the same at a set time every year: that they used to catch a Greek foreigner, and fat him thus up every year, and then lead him to a certain wood, and kill him, and sacrifice with their accustomed solemnities, and taste of his entrails, and take an oath upon this sacrificing a Greek, that they would ever be at enmity with the Greeks; and that then they threw the remaining parts of the miserable wretch into a certain pit." Apion adds further, that, "the man said there were but a few days to come ere he was to be slain, and implored of Antiochus that, out of the reverence he bore to the Grecian gods, he would disappoint the snares the Jews laid for his blood, and would deliver him from the miseries with which he was encompassed." [11] Now this is such a most tragical fable as is full of nothing but cruelty and impudence; yet does it not excuse Antiochus of his sacrilegious attempt, as those who write it in his vindication are willing to suppose; for he could not presume beforehand that he should meet with any such thing in coming to the temple, but must have found it unexpectedly. He was therefore still an impious person, that was given to unlawful pleasures, and had no regard to God in his actions. But [as for Apion], he hath done whatever his extravagant love of lying hath dictated to him, as it is most easy to discover by a consideration of his writings; for the difference of our laws is known not to regard the Grecians only, but they are principally opposite to the Egyptians, and to some other nations also for while it so falls out that men of all countries come sometimes and sojourn among us, how comes it about that we take an oath, and conspire only against the Grecians, and that by the effusion of their blood also? Or how is it possible that all the Jews should get together to these sacrifices, and the entrails of one man should be sufficient for so many thousands to taste of them, as Apion pretends? Or why did not the king carry this man, whosoever he was, and whatsoever was his name, [which is not set down in Apion's book,] with great pomp back into his own country? when he might thereby have been esteemed a religious person himself, and a mighty lover of the Greeks, and might thereby have procured himself great assistance from all men against that hatred the Jews bore to him. But I leave this matter; for the proper way of confuting fools is not to use bare words, but to appeal to the things themselves that make against them. Now, then, all such as ever saw the construction of our temple, of what nature it was, know well enough how the purity of it was never to be profaned; for it had four several courts [12] encompassed with cloisters round about, every one of which had by our law a peculiar degree of separation from the rest. Into the first court every body was allowed to go, even foreigners, and none but women, during their courses, were prohibited to pass through it; all the Jews went into the second court, as well as their wives, when they were free from all uncleanness; into the third court went in the Jewish men, when they were clean and purified; into the fourth went the priests, having on their sacerdotal garments; but for the most sacred place, none went in but the high priests, clothed in their peculiar garments. Now there is so great caution used about these offices of religion, that the priests are appointed to go into the temple but at certain hours; for in the morning, at the opening of the inner temple, those that are to officiate receive the sacrifices, as they do again at noon, till the doors are shut. Lastly, it is not so much as lawful to carry any vessel into the holy house; nor is there any thing therein, but the altar [of incense], the table [of shew-bread], the censer, and the candlestick, which are all written in the law; for there is nothing further there, nor are there any mysteries performed that may not be spoken of; nor is there any feasting within the place. For what I have now said is publicly known, and supported by the testimony of the whole people, and their operations are very manifest; for although there be four courses of the priests, and every one of them have above five thousand men in them, yet do they officiate on certain days only; and when those days are over, other priests succeed in the performance of their sacrifices, and assemble together at mid-day, and receive the keys of the temple, and the vessels by tale, without any thing relating to food or drink being carried into the temple; nay, we are not allowed to offer such things at the altar, excepting what is prepared for the sacrifices.

9. What then can we say of Apion, but that he examined nothing that concerned these things, while still he uttered incredible words about them? but it is a great shame for a grammarian not to be able to write true history. Now if he knew the purity of our temple, he hath entirely omitted to take notice of it; but he forges a story about the seizing of a Grecian, about ineffable food, and the most delicious preparation of dainties; and pretends that strangers could go into a place whereinto the noblest men among the Jews are not allowed to enter, unless they be priests. This, therefore, is the utmost degree of impiety, and a voluntary lie, in order to the delusion of those who will not examine into the truth of matters; whereas such unspeakable mischiefs as are above related have been occasioned by such calumnies that are raised upon us.

10. Nay, this miracle or piety derides us further, and adds the following pretended facts to his former fable; for he says that this man related how, "while the Jews were once in a long war with the Idumeans, there came a man out of one of the cities of the Idumeans, who there had worshipped Apollo. This man, whose name is said to have been Zabidus, came to the Jews, and promised that he would deliver Apollo, the god of Dora, into their hands, and that he would come to our temple, if they would all come up with him, and bring the whole multitude of the Jews with them; that Zabidus made him a certain wooden instrument, and put it round about him, and set three rows of lamps therein, and walked after such a manner, that he appeared to those that stood a great way off him to be a kind of star, walking upon the earth; that the Jews were terribly affrighted at so surprising an appearance, and stood very quiet at a distance; and that Zabidus, while they continued so very quiet, went into the holy house, and carried off that golden head of an ass, [for so facetiously does he write,] and then went his way back again to Dora in great haste." And say you so, sir! as I may reply; then does Apion load the ass, that is, himself, and lays on him a burden of fooleries and lies; for he writes of places that have no being, and not knowing the cities he speaks of, he changes their situation; for Idumea borders upon our country, and is near to Gaza, in which there is no such city as Dora; although there be, it is true, a city named Dora in Phoenicia, near Mount Carmel, but it is four days' journey from Idumea. Now, then, why does this man accuse us, because we have not gods in common with other nations, if our fathers were so easily prevailed upon to have Apollo come to them, and thought they saw him walking upon the earth, and the stars

with him? for certainly those who have so many festivals, wherein they light lamps, must yet, at this rate, have never seen a candlestick! But still it seems that while Zabidus took his journey over the country, where were so many ten thousands of people, nobody met him. He also, it seems, even in a time of war, found the walls of Jerusalem destitute of guards. I omit the rest. Now the doors of the holy house were seventy [13] cubits high, and twenty cubits broad; they were all plated over with gold, and almost of solid gold itself, and there were no fewer than twenty [14] men required to shut them every day; nor was it lawful ever to leave them open, though it seems this lamp-bearer of ours opened them easily, or thought he opened them, as he thought he had the ass's head in his hand. Whether, therefore, he returned it to us again, or whether Apion took it, and brought it into the temple again, that Antiochus might find it, and afford a handle for a second fable of Apion's, is uncertain.

11. Apion also tells a false story, when he mentions an oath of ours, as if we "swore by God, the Maker of the heaven, and earth, and sea, to bear no good will to any foreigner, and particularly to none of the Greeks." Now this liar ought to have said directly that, "we would bear no good-will to any foreigner, and particularly to none of the Egyptians." For then his story about the oath would have squared with the rest of his original forgeries, in case our forefathers had been driven away by their kinsmen, the Egyptians, not on account of any wickedness they had been guilty of, but on account of the calamities they were under; for as to the Grecians, we were rather remote from them in place, than different from them in our institutions, insomuch that we have no enmity with them, nor any jealousy of them. On the contrary, it hath so happened that many of them have come over to our laws, and some of them have continued in their observation, although others of them had not courage enough to persevere, and so departed from them again; nor did any body ever hear this oath sworn by us: Apion, it seems, was the only person that heard it, for he indeed was the first composer of it.

12. However, Apion deserves to be admired for his great prudence, as to what I am going to say, which is this, "That there is a plain mark among us, that we neither have just laws, nor worship God as we ought to do, because we are not governors, but are rather in subjection to Gentiles, sometimes to one nation, and sometimes to another; and that our city hath been liable to several calamities, while their city [Alexandria] hath been of old time an imperial city, and not used to be in subjection to the Romans." But now this man had better leave off this bragging, for every body but himself would think that Apion said what he hath said against himself; for there are very few nations that have had the good fortune

to continue many generations in the principality, but still the mutations in human affairs have put them into subjection under others; and most nations have been often subdued, and brought into subjection by others. Now for the Egyptians, perhaps they are the only nation that have had this extraordinary privilege, to have never served any of those monarchs who subdued Asia and Europe, and this on account, as they pretend, that the gods fled into their country, and saved themselves by being changed into the shapes of wild beasts! Whereas these Egyptians [15] are the very people that appear to have never, in all the past ages, had one day of freedom, no, not so much as from their own lords. For I will not reproach them with relating the manner how the Persians used them, and this not once only, but many times, when they laid their cities waste, demolished their temples, and cut the throats of those animals whom they esteemed to be gods; for it is not reasonable to imitate the clownish ignorance of Apion, who hath no regard to the misfortunes of the Athenians, or of the Lacedemonians, the latter of whom were styled by all men the most courageous, and the former the most religious of the Grecians. I say nothing of such kings as have been famous for piety, particularly of one of them, whose name was Cresus, nor what calamities he met with in his life; I say nothing of the citadel of Athens, of the temple at Ephesus, of that at Delphi, nor of ten thousand others which have been burnt down, while nobody cast reproaches on those that were the sufferers, but on those that were the actors therein. But now we have met with Apion, an accuser of our nation, though one that still forgets the miseries of his own people, the Egyptians; but it is that Sesostris who was once so celebrated a king of Egypt that hath blinded him. Now we will not brag of our kings, David and Solomon, though they conquered many nations; accordingly we will let them alone. However, Apion is ignorant of what every body knows, that the Egyptians were servants to the Persians, and afterwards to the Macedonians, when they were lords of Asia, and were no better than slaves, while we have enjoyed liberty formerly; nay, more than that, have had the dominion of the cities that lie round about us, and this nearly for a hundred and twenty years together, until Pompeius Magnus. And when all the kings every where were conquered by the Romans, our ancestors were the only people who continued to be esteemed their confederates and friends, on account of their fidelity to them.[16]

13. "But," says Apion, "we Jews have not had any wonderful men amongst us, not any inventors of arts, nor any eminent for wisdom." He then enumerates Socrates, and Zeno, and Cleanthes, and some others of the same sort; and, after all, he adds himself to them, which is the most wonderful thing of all that he says, and pronounces Alexandria to be happy, because it hath such a citizen as he is in

it; for he was the fittest man to be a witness to his own deserts, although he hath appeared to all others no better than a wicked mountebank, of a corrupt life and ill discourses; on which account one may justly pity Alexandria, if it should value itself upon such a citizen as he is. But as to our own men, we have had those who have been as deserving of commendation as any other whosoever, and such as have perused our Antiquities cannot be ignorant of them.

14. As to the other things which he sets down as blameworthy, it may perhaps be the best way to let them pass without apology, that he may be allowed to be his own accuser, and the accuser of the rest of the Egyptians. However, he accuses us for sacrificing animals, and for abstaining from swine's flesh, and laughs at us for the circumcision of our privy members. Now as for our slaughter of tame animals for sacrifices, it is common to us and to all other men; but this Apion, by making it a crime to sacrifice them, demonstrates himself to be an Egyptian; for had he been either a Grecian or a Macedonian, [as he pretends to be,] he had not shown any uneasiness at it; for those people glory in sacrificing whole hecatombs to the gods, and make use of those sacrifices for feasting; and yet is not the world thereby rendered destitute of cattle, as Apion was afraid would come to pass. Yet if all men had followed the manners of the Egyptians, the world had certainly been made desolate as to mankind, but had been filled full of the wildest sort of brute beasts, which, because they suppose them to be gods, they carefully nourish. However, if any one should ask Apion which of the Egyptians he thinks to be the most wise and most pious of them all, he would certainly acknowledge the priests to be so; for the histories say that two things were originally committed to their care by their kings' injunctions, the worship of the gods, and the support of wisdom and philosophy. Accordingly, these priests are all circumcised, and abstain from swine's flesh; nor does any one of the other Egyptians assist them in slaying those sacrifices they offer to the gods. Apion was therefore quite blinded in his mind, when, for the sake of the Egyptians, he contrived to reproach us, and to accuse such others as not only make use of that conduct of life which he so much abuses, but have also taught other men to be circumcised, as says Herodotus; which makes me think that Apion is hereby justly punished for his casting such reproaches on the laws of his own country; for he was circumcised himself of necessity, on account of an ulcer in his privy member; and when he received no benefit by such circumcision, but his member became putrid, he died in great torment. Now men of good tempers ought to observe their own laws concerning religion accurately, and to persevere therein, but not presently to abuse the laws of other nations, while this Apion deserted his own laws, and told lies about ours. And this was the end of Apion's life, and this shall be the conclusion of our discourse about him.

15. But now, since Apollonius Molo, and Lysimachus, and some others, write treatises about our lawgiver Moses, and about our laws, which are neither just nor true, and this partly out of ignorance, but chiefly out of ill-will to us, while they calumniate Moses as an impostor and deceiver, and pretend that our laws teach us wickedness, but nothing that is virtuous, I have a mind to discourse briefly, according to my ability, about our whole constitution of government, and about the particular branches of it. For I suppose it will thence become evident, that the laws we have given us are disposed after the best manner for the advancement of piety, for mutual communion with one another, for a general love of mankind, as also for justice, and for sustaining labors with fortitude, and for a contempt of death. And I beg of those that shall peruse this writing of mine, to read it without partiality; for it is not my purpose to write an encomium upon ourselves, but I shall esteem this as a most just apology for us, and taken from those our laws, according to which we lead our lives, against the many and the lying objections that have been made against us. Moreover, since this Apollonius does not do like Apion, and lay a continued accusation against us, but does it only by starts, and up and down his discourse, while he sometimes reproaches us as atheists, and man-haters, and sometimes hits us in the teeth with our want of courage, and yet sometimes, on the contrary, accuses us of too great boldness and madness in our conduct; nay, he says that we are the weakest of all the barbarians, and that this is the reason why we are the only people who have made no improvements in human life; now I think I shall have then sufficiently disproved all these his allegations, when it shall appear that our laws enjoin the very reverse of what he says, and that we very carefully observe those laws ourselves. And if I be compelled to make mention of the laws of other nations, that are contrary to ours, those ought deservedly to thank themselves for it, who have pretended to depreciate our laws in comparison of their own; nor will there, I think, be any room after that for them to pretend either that we have no such laws ourselves, an epitome of which I will present to the reader, or that we do not, above all men, continue in the observation of them.

16. To begin then a good way backward, I would advance this, in the first place, that those who have been admirers of good order, and of living under common laws, and who began to introduce them, may well have this testimony that they are better than other men, both for moderation and such virtue as is agreeable to nature. Indeed their endeavor was to have every thing they ordained believed to be very ancient, that they might not be thought to imitate others, but might appear to have delivered a regular way of living to others after them. Since then this is the case, the excellency of a legislator is seen in providing for the

people's living after the best manner, and in prevailing with those that are to use the laws he ordains for them, to have a good opinion of them, and in obliging the multitude to persevere in them, and to make no changes in them, neither in prosperity nor adversity. Now I venture to say, that our legislator is the most ancient of all the legislators whom we have ally where heard of; for as for the Lycurguses, and Solons, and Zaleucus Locrensis, and all those legislators who are so admired by the Greeks, they seem to be of yesterday, if compared with our legislator, insomuch as the very name of a law was not so much as known in old times among the Grecians. Homer is a witness to the truth of this observation, who never uses that term in all his poems; for indeed there was then no such thing among them, but the multitude was governed by wise maxims, and by the injunctions of their king. It was also a long time that they continued in the use of these unwritten customs, although they were always changing them upon several occasions. But for our legislator, who was of so much greater antiquity than the rest, [as even those that speak against us upon all occasions do always confess,] he exhibited himself to the people as their best governor and counselor, and included in his legislation the entire conduct of their lives, and prevailed with them to receive it, and brought it so to pass, that those that were made acquainted with his laws did most carefully observe them.

17. But let us consider his first and greatest work; for when it was resolved on by our forefathers to leave Egypt, and return to their own country, this Moses took the many tell thousands that were of the people, and saved them out of many desperate distresses, and brought them home in safety. And certainly it was here necessary to travel over a country without water, and full of sand, to overcome their enemies, and, during these battles, to preserve their children, and their wives, and their prey; on all which occasions he became an excellent general of an army, and a most prudent counselor, and one that took the truest care of them all; he also so brought it about, that the whole multitude depended upon him. And while he had them always obedient to what he enjoined, he made no manner of use of his authority for his own private advantage, which is the usual time when governors gain great powers to themselves, and pave the way for tyranny, and accustom the multitude to live very dissolutely; whereas, when our legislator was in so great authority, he, on the contrary, thought he ought to have regard to piety, and to show his great good-will to the people; and by this means he thought he might show the great degree of virtue that was in him, and might procure the most lasting security to those who had made him their governor. When he had therefore come to such a good resolution, and had performed such wonderful exploits, we had just reason to look upon ourselves as having him for a divine

governor and counselor. And when he had first persuaded himself [17] that his actions and designs were agreeable to God's will, he thought it his duty to impress, above all things, that notion upon the multitude; for those who have once believed that God is the inspector of their lives, will not permit themselves in any sin. And this is the character of our legislator: he was no impostor, no deceiver, as his revilers say, though unjustly, but such a one as they brag Minos [18] to have been among the Greeks, and other legislators after him; for some of them suppose that they had their laws from Jupiter, while Minos said that the revelation of his laws was to be referred to Apollo, and his oracle at Delphi, whether they really thought they were so derived, or supposed, however, that they could persuade the people easily that so it was. But which of these it was who made the best laws, and which had the greatest reason to believe that God was their author, it will be easy, upon comparing those laws themselves together, to determine; for it is time that we come to that point. [19] Now there are innumerable differences in the particular customs and laws that are among all mankind, which a man may briefly reduce under the following heads: Some legislators have permitted their governments to be under monarchies, others put them under oligarchies, and others under a republican form; but our legislator had no regard to any of these forms, but he ordained our government to be what, by a strained expression, may be termed a Theocracy, [20] by ascribing the authority and the power to God, and by persuading all the people to have a regard to him, as the author of all the good things that were enjoyed either in common by all mankind, or by each one in particular, and of all that they themselves obtained by praying to him in their greatest difficulties. He informed them that it was impossible to escape God's observation, even in any of our outward actions, or in any of our inward thoughts. Moreover, he represented God as unbegotten, [21] and immutable, through all eternity, superior to all mortal conceptions in pulchritude; and, though known to us by his power, yet unknown to us as to his essence. I do not now explain how these notions of God are the sentiments of the wisest among the Grecians, and how they were taught them upon the principles that he afforded them. However, they testify, with great assurance, that these notions are just, and agreeable to the nature of God, and to his majesty; for Pythagoras, and Anaxagoras, and Plato, and the Stoic philosophers that succeeded them, and almost all the rest, are of the same sentiments, and had the same notions of the nature of God; yet durst not these men disclose those true notions to more than a few, because the body of the people were prejudiced with other opinions beforehand. But our legislator, who made his actions agree to his laws, did not only prevail with those that were his contemporaries to agree with these his notions, but so firmly imprinted this faith in God upon all their posterity, that it never could be removed. The reason why the constitution of this legislation was ever better directed to the utility of all than other legislations were, is this, that Moses did not make religion a part of virtue, but he saw and he ordained other virtues to be parts of religion; I mean justice, and fortitude, and temperance, and a universal agreement of the members of the community with one another; for all our actions and studies, and all our words, [in Moses's settlement,] have a reference to piety towards God; for he hath left none of these in suspense, or undetermined. For there are two ways of coming at any sort of learning and a moral conduct of life; the one is by instruction in words, the other by practical exercises. Now other lawgivers have separated these two ways in their opinions, and choosing one of those ways of instruction, or that which best pleased every one of them, neglected the other. Thus did the Lacedemonians and the Cretians teach by practical exercises, but not by words; while the Athenians, and almost all the other Grecians, made laws about what was to be done, or left undone, but had no regard to the exercising them thereto in practice.

18. But for our legislator, he very carefully joined these two methods of instruction together; for he neither left these practical exercises to go on without verbal instruction, nor did he permit the hearing of the law to proceed without the exercises for practice; but beginning immediately from the earliest infancy, and the appointment of every one's diet, he left nothing of the very smallest consequence to be done at the pleasure and disposal of the person himself. Accordingly, he made a fixed rule of law what sorts of food they should abstain from, and what sorts they should make use of; as also, what communion they should have with others what great diligence they should use in their occupations, and what times of rest should be interposed, that, by living under that law as under a father and a master, we might be guilty of no sin, neither voluntary nor out of ignorance; for he did not suffer the guilt of ignorance to go on without punishment, but demonstrated the law to be the best and the most necessary instruction of all others, permitting the people to leave off their other employments, and to assemble together for the hearing of the law, and learning it exactly, and this not once or twice, or oftener, but every week; which thing all the other legislators seem to have neglected.

19. And indeed the greatest part of mankind are so far from living according to their own laws, that they hardly know them; but when they have sinned, they learn from others that they have transgressed the law. Those also who are in the highest and principal posts of the government, confess they are not acquainted with those laws, and are obliged to take such persons for their assessors in public administrations as profess to have skill in those laws; but for our people, if any

body do but ask any one of them about our laws, he will more readily tell them all than he will tell his own name, and this in consequence of our having learned them immediately as soon as ever we became sensible of any thing, and of our having them as it were engraven on our souls. Our transgressors of them are but few, and it is impossible, when any do offend, to escape punishment.

20. And this very thing it is that principally creates such a wonderful agreement of minds amongst us all; for this entire agreement of ours in all our notions concerning God, and our having no difference in our course of life and manners, procures among us the most excellent concord of these our manners that is any where among mankind; for no other people but the Jews have avoided all discourses about God that any way contradict one another, which yet are frequent among other nations; and this is true not only among ordinary persons, according as every one is affected, but some of the philosophers have been insolent enough to indulge such contradictions, while some of them have undertaken to use such words as entirely take away the nature of God, as others of them have taken away his providence over mankind. Nor can any one perceive amongst us any difference in the conduct of our lives, but all our works are common to us all. We have one sort of discourse concerning God, which is conformable to our law, and affirms that he sees all things; as also we have but one way of speaking concerning the conduct of our lives, that all other things ought to have piety for their end; and this any body may hear from our women, and servants themselves.

21. And, indeed, hence hath arisen that accusation which some make against us, that we have not produced men that have been the inventors of new operations, or of new ways of speaking; for others think it a fine thing to persevere in nothing that has been delivered down from their forefathers, and these testify it to be an instance of the sharpest wisdom when these men venture to transgress those traditions; whereas we, on the contrary, suppose it to be our only wisdom and virtue to admit no actions nor supposals that are contrary to our original laws; which procedure of ours is a just and sure sign that our law is admirably constituted; for such laws as are not thus well made are convicted upon trial to want amendment.

22. But while we are ourselves persuaded that our law was made agreeably to the will of God, it would be impious for us not to observe the same; for what is there in it that any body would change? and what can be invented that is better? or what can we take out of other people's laws that will exceed it? Perhaps some would have the entire settlement of our government altered. And where shall we find a better or more righteous constitution than ours, while this makes us esteem

God to be the Governor of the universe, and permits the priests in general to be the administrators of the principal affairs, and withal intrusts the government over the other priests to the chief high priest himself? which priests our legislator, at their first appointment, did not advance to that dignity for their riches, or any abundance of other possessions, or any plenty they had as the gifts of fortune; but he intrusted the principal management of Divine worship to those that exceeded others in an ability to persuade men, and in prudence of conduct. These men had the main care of the law and of the other parts of the people's conduct committed to them; for they were the priests who were ordained to be the inspectors of all, and the judges in doubtful cases, and the punishers of those that were condemned to suffer punishment.

23. What form of government then can be more holy than this? what more worthy kind of worship can be paid to God than we pay, where the entire body of the people are prepared for religion, where an extraordinary degree of care is required in the priests, and where the whole polity is so ordered as if it were a certain religious solemnity? For what things foreigners, when they solemnize such festivals, are not able to observe for a few days' time, and call them Mysteries and Sacred Ceremonies, we observe with great pleasure and an unshaken resolution during our whole lives. What are the things then that we are commanded or forbidden? They are simple, and easily known. The first command is concerning God, and affirms that God contains all things, and is a Being every way perfect and happy, self-sufficient, and supplying all other beings; the beginning, the middle, and the end of all things. He is manifest in his works and benefits, and more conspicuous than any other being whatsoever; but as to his form and magnitude, he is most obscure. All materials, let them be ever so costly, are unworthy to compose an image for him, and all arts are unartful to express the notion we ought to have of him. We can neither see nor think of any thing like him, nor is it agreeable to piety to form a resemblance of him. We see his works, the light, the heaven, the earth, the sun and the moon, the waters, the generations of animals, the productions of fruits. These things hath God made, not with hands, nor with labor, nor as wanting the assistance of any to cooperate with him; but as his will resolved they should be made and be good also, they were made and became good immediately. All men ought to follow this Being, and to worship him in the exercise of virtue; for this way of worship of God is the most holy of all others.

24. There ought also to be but one temple for one God; for likeness is the constant foundation of agreement. This temple ought to be common to all men, because he is the common God of all men. High priests are to be continually

about his worship, over whom he that is the first by his birth is to be their ruler perpetually. His business must be to offer sacrifices to God, together with those priests that are joined with him, to see that the laws be observed, to determine controversies, and to punish those that are convicted of injustice; while he that does not submit to him shall be subject to the same punishment, as if he had been guilty of impiety towards God himself. When we offer sacrifices to him, we do it not in order to surfeit ourselves, or to be drunken; for such excesses are against the will of God, and would be an occasion of injuries and of luxury; but by keeping ourselves sober, orderly, and ready for our other occupations, and being more temperate than others. And for our duty at the sacrifices [22] themselves, we ought, in the first place, to pray for the common welfare of all, and after that for our own; for we are made for fellowship one with another, and he who prefers the common good before what is peculiar to himself is above all acceptable to God. And let our prayers and supplications be made humbly to God, not [so much] that he would give us what is good, [for he hath already given that of his own accord, and hath proposed the same publicly to all,] as that we may duly receive it, and when we have received it, may preserve it. Now the law has appointed several purifications at our sacrifices, whereby we are cleansed after a funeral, after what sometimes happens to us in bed, and after accompanying with our wives, and upon many other occasions, which it would be too long now to set down. And this is our doctrine concerning God and his worship, and is the same that the law appoints for our practice.

25. But, then, what are our laws about marriage? That law owns no other mixture of sexes but that which nature hath appointed, of a man with his wife, and that this be used only for the procreation of children. But it abhors the mixture of a male with a male; and if any one do that, death is its punishment. It commands us also, when we marry, not to have regard to portion, nor to take a woman by violence, nor to persuade her deceitfully and knavishly; but to demand her in marriage of him who hath power to dispose of her, and is fit to give her away by the nearness of his kindred; for, says the Scripture, "A woman is inferior to her husband in all things."[23] Let her, therefore, be obedient to him; not so that he should abuse her, but that she may acknowledge her duty to her husband; for God hath given the authority to the husband. A husband, therefore, is to lie only with his wife whom he hath married; but to have to do with another man's wife is a wicked thing, which, if any one ventures upon, death is inevitably his punishment: no more can he avoid the same who forces a virgin betrothed to another man, or entices another man's wife. The law, moreover, enjoins us to bring up all our offspring, and forbids women to cause abortion of what is

begotten, or to destroy it afterward; and if any woman appears to have so done, she will be a murderer of her child, by destroying a living creature, and diminishing human kind; if any one, therefore, proceeds to such fornication or murder, he cannot be clean. Moreover, the law enjoins, that after the man and wife have lain together in a regular way, they shall bathe themselves; for there is a defilement contracted thereby, both in soul and body, as if they had gone into another country; for indeed the soul, by being united to the body, is subject to miseries, and is not freed therefrom again but by death; on which account the law requires this purification to be entirely performed.

26. Nay, indeed, the law does not permit us to make festivals at the births of our children, and thereby afford occasion of drinking to excess; but it ordains that the very beginning of our education should be immediately directed to sobriety. It also commands us to bring those children up in learning, and to exercise them in the laws, and make them acquainted with the acts of their predecessors, in order to their imitation of them, and that they might be nourished up in the laws from their infancy, and might neither transgress them, nor have any pretense for their ignorance of them.

27. Our law hath also taken care of the decent burial of the dead, but without any extravagant expenses for their funerals, and without the erection of any illustrious monuments for them; but hath ordered that their nearest relations should perform their obsequies; and hath showed it to be regular, that all who pass by when any one is buried should accompany the funeral, and join in the lamentation. It also ordains that the house and its inhabitants should be purified after the funeral is over, that every one may thence learn to keep at a great distance from the thoughts of being pure, if he hath been once guilty of murder.

28. The law ordains also, that parents should be honored immediately after God himself, and delivers that son who does not requite them for the benefits he hath received from them, but is deficient on any such occasion, to be stoned. It also says that the young men should pay due respect to every elder, since God is the eldest of all beings. It does not give leave to conceal any thing from our friends, because that is not true friendship which will not commit all things to their fidelity: it also forbids the revelation of secrets, even though an enmity arise between them. If any judge takes bribes, his punishment is death: he that overlooks one that offers him a petition, and this when he is able to relieve him, he is a guilty person. What is not by any one intrusted to another ought not to be required back again. No one is to touch another's goods. He that lends money must not demand usury for its loan. These, and many more of the like sort, are the rules that unite us in the bands of society one with another.

29. It will be also worth our while to see what equity our legislator would have us exercise in our intercourse with strangers; for it will thence appear that he made the best provision he possibly could, both that we should not dissolve our own constitution, nor show any envious mind towards those that would cultivate a friendship with us. Accordingly, our legislator admits all those that have a mind to observe our laws so to do; and this after a friendly manner, as esteeming that a true union which not only extends to our own stock, but to those that would live after the same manner with us; yet does he not allow those that come to us by accident only to be admitted into communion with us.

30. However, there are other things which our legislator ordained for us beforehand, which of necessity we ought to do in common to all men; as to afford fire, and water, and food to such as want it; to show them the roads; not to let any one lie unburied. He also would have us treat those that are esteemed our enemies with moderation; for he doth not allow us to set their country on fire, nor permit us to cut down those trees that bear fruit; nay, further, he forbids us to spoil those that have been slain in war. He hath also provided for such as are taken captive, that they may not be injured, and especially that the women may not be abused. Indeed he hath taught us gentleness and humanity so effectually, that he hath not despised the care of brute beasts, by permitting no other than a regular use of them, and forbidding any other; and if any of them come to our houses, like supplicants, we are forbidden to slay them; nor may we kill the dams, together with their young ones; but we are obliged, even in an enemy's country, to spare and not kill those creatures that labor for mankind. Thus hath our lawgiver contrived to teach us an equitable conduct every way, by using us to such laws as instruct us therein; while at the same time he hath ordained that such as break these laws should be punished, without the allowance of any excuse whatsoever.

31. Now the greatest part of offenses with us are capital; as if any one be guilty of adultery; if any one force a virgin; if any one be so impudent as to attempt sodomy with a male; or if, upon another's making an attempt upon him, he submits to be so used. There is also a law for slaves of the like nature, that can never be avoided. Moreover, if any one cheats another in measures or weights, or makes a knavish bargain and sale, in order to cheat another; if any one steals what belongs to another, and takes what he never deposited; all these have punishments allotted them; not such as are met with among other nations, but more severe ones. And as for attempts of unjust behavior towards parents, or for impiety against God, though they be not actually accomplished, the offenders are destroyed immediately. However, the reward for such as live exactly according to the laws is not silver or gold; it is not a garland of olive branches or of small age,

nor any such public sign of commendation; but every good man hath his own conscience bearing witness to himself, and by virtue of our legislator's prophetic spirit, and of the firm security God himself affords such a one, he believes that God hath made this grant to those that observe these laws, even though they be obliged readily to die for them, that they shall come into being again, and at a certain revolution of things shall receive a better life than they had enjoyed before. Nor would I venture to write thus at this time, were it not well known to all by our actions that many of our people have many a time bravely resolved to endure any sufferings, rather than speak one word against our law.

32. Nay, indeed, in case it had so fallen out, that our nation had not been so thoroughly known among all men as they are, and our voluntary submission to our laws had not been so open and manifest as it is, but that somebody had pretended to have written these laws himself, and had read them to the Greeks, or had pretended that he had met with men out of the limits of the known world, that had such reverent notions of God, and had continued a long time in the firm observance of such laws as ours, I cannot but suppose that all men would admire them on a reflection upon the frequent changes they had therein been themselves subject to; and this while those that have attempted to write somewhat of the same kind for politic government, and for laws, are accused as composing monstrous things, and are said to have undertaken an impossible task upon them. And here I will say nothing of those other philosophers who have undertaken any thing of this nature in their writings. But even Plato himself, who is so admired by the Greeks on account of that gravity in his manners, and force in his words, and that ability he had to persuade men beyond all other philosophers, is little better than laughed at and exposed to ridicule on that account, by those that pretend to sagacity in political affairs; although he that shall diligently peruse his writings will find his precepts to be somewhat gentle, and pretty near to the customs of the generality of mankind. Nay, Plato himself confesseth that it is not safe to publish the true notion concerning God among the ignorant multitude. Yet do some men look upon Plato's discourses as no better than certain idle words set off with great artifice. However, they admire Lycurgus as the principal lawgiver, and all men celebrate Sparta for having continued in the firm observance of his laws for a very long time. So far then we have gained, that it is to be confessed a mark of virtue to submit to laws. [24] But then let such as admire this in the Lacedemonians compare that duration of theirs with more than two thousand years which our political government hath continued; and let them further consider, that though the Lacedemonians did seem to observe their laws exactly while they enjoyed their liberty, yet that when they underwent a change of their fortune, they forgot almost

all those laws; while we, having been under ten thousand changes in our fortune by the changes that happened among the kings of Asia, have never betrayed our laws under the most pressing distresses we have been in; nor have we neglected them either out of sloth or for a livelihood. [25] if any one will consider it, the difficulties and labors laid upon us have been greater than what appears to have been borne by the Lacedemonian fortitude, while they neither ploughed their land, nor exercised any trades, but lived in their own city, free from all such pains-taking, in the enjoyment of plenty, and using such exercises as might improve their bodies, while they made use of other men as their servants for all the necessaries of life, and had their food prepared for them by the others; and these good and humane actions they do for no other purpose but this, that by their actions and their sufferings they may be able to conquer all those against whom they make war. I need not add this, that they have not been fully able to observe their laws; for not only a few single persons, but multitudes of them, have in heaps neglected those laws, and have delivered themselves, together with their arms, into the hands of their enemies.

33. Now as for ourselves, I venture to say that no one can tell of so many; nay, not of more than one or two that have betrayed our laws, no, not out of fear of death itself; I do not mean such an easy death as happens in battles, but that which comes with bodily torments, and seems to be the severest kind of death of all others. Now I think those that have conquered us have put us to such deaths, not out of their hatred to us when they had subdued us, but rather out of their desire of seeing a surprising sight, which is this, whether there be such men in the world who believe that no evil is to them so great as to be compelled to do or to speak any thing contrary to their own laws. Nor ought men to wonder at us, if we are more courageous in dying for our laws than all other men are; for other men do not easily submit to the easier things in which we are instituted; I mean working with our hands, and eating but little, and being contented to eat and drink, not at random, or at every one's pleasure, or being under inviolable rules in lying with our wives, in magnificent furniture, and again in the observation of our times of rest; while those that can use their swords in war, and can put their enemies to flight when they attack them, cannot bear to submit to such laws about their way of living: whereas our being accustomed willingly to submit to laws in these instances, renders us fit to show our fortitude upon other occasions also.

34. Yet do the Lysimachi and the Molones, and some other writers, [unskillful sophists as they are, and the deceivers of young men,] reproach us as the vilest of all mankind. Now I have no mind to make an inquiry into the laws of other nations; for the custom of our country is to keep our own laws, but not to bring

accusations against the laws of others. And indeed our legislator hath expressly forbidden us to laugh at and revile those that are esteemed gods by other people? on account of the very name of God ascribed to them. But since our antagonists think to run us down upon the comparison of their religion and ours, it is not possible to keep silence here, especially while what I shall say to confute these men will not be now first said, but hath been already said by many, and these of the highest reputation also; for who is there among those that have been admired among the Greeks for wisdom, who hath not greatly blamed both the most famous poets, and most celebrated legislators, for spreading such notions originally among the body of the people concerning the gods? such as these, that they may be allowed to be as numerous as they have a mind to have them; that they are begotten one by another, and that after all the kinds of generation you can imagine. They also distinguish them in their places and ways of living as they would distinguish several sorts of animals; as some to be under the earth; as some to be in the sea; and the ancientest of them all to be bound in hell; and for those to whom they have allotted heaven, they have set over them one, who in title is their father, but in his actions a tyrant and a lord; whence it came to pass that his wife, and brother, and daughter [which daughter he brought forth from his own head] made a conspiracy against him to seize upon him and confine hint, as he had himself seized upon and confined his own father before.

35. And justly have the wisest men thought these notions deserved severe rebukes; they also laugh at them for determining that we ought to believe some of the gods to be beardless and young, and others of them to be old, and to have beards accordingly; that some are set to trades; that one god is a smith, and another goddess is a weaver; that one god is a warrior, and fights with men; that some of them are harpers, or delight in archery; and besides, that mutual seditions arise among them, and that they quarrel about men, and this so far, that they not only lay hands upon one another, but that they are wounded by men, and lament, and take on for such their afflictions. But what is the grossest of all in point of lasciviousness, are those unbounded lusts ascribed to almost all of them, and their amours; which how can it be other than a most absurd supposal, especially when it reaches to the male gods, and to the female goddesses also? Moreover, the chief of all their gods, and their first father himself, overlooks those goddesses whom he hath deluded and begotten with child, and suffers them to be kept in prison, or drowned in the sea. He is also so bound up by fate, that he cannot save his own offspring, nor can he bear their deaths without shedding of tears. These are fine things indeed! as are the rest that follow. Adulteries truly are so impudently looked on in heaven by the gods, that some of them have confessed they envied those

that were found in the very act. And why should they not do so, when the eldest of them, who is their king also, hath not been able to restrain himself in the violence of his lust, from lying with his wife, so long as they might get into their bedchamber? Now some of the gods are servants to men, and will sometimes be builders for a reward, and sometimes will be shepherds; while others of them, like malefactors, are bound in a prison of brass. And what sober person is there who would not be provoked at such stories, and rebuke those that forged them, and condemn the great silliness of those that admit them for true? Nay, others there are that have advanced a certain timorousness and fear, as also madness and fraud, and any other of the vilest passions, into the nature and form of gods, and have persuaded whole cities to offer sacrifices to the better sort of them; on which account they have been absolutely forced to esteem some gods as the givers of good things, and to call others of them averters of evil. They also endeavor to move them, as they would the vilest of men, by gifts and presents, as looking for nothing else than to receive some great mischief from them, unless they pay them such wages.

36. Wherefore it deserves our inquiry what should be the occasion of this unjust management, and of these scandals about the Deity. And truly I suppose it to be derived from the imperfect knowledge the heathen legislators had at first of the true nature of God; nor did they explain to the people even so far as they did comprehend of it: nor did they compose the other parts of their political settlements according to it, but omitted it as a thing of very little consequence, and gave leave both to the poets to introduce what gods they pleased, and those subject to all sorts of passions, and to the orators to procure political decrees from the people for the admission of such foreign gods as they thought proper. The painters also, and statuaries of Greece, had herein great power, as each of them could contrive a shape [proper for a god]; the one to be formed out of clay, and the other by making a bare picture of such a one. But those workmen that were principally admired, had the use of ivory and of gold as the constant materials for their new statues [whereby it comes to pass that some temples are quite deserted, while others are in great esteem, and adorned with all the rites of all kinds of purification]. Besides this, the first gods, who have long flourished in the honors done them, are now grown old [while those that flourished after them are come in their room as a second rank, that I may speak the most honorably of them I can]: nay, certain other gods there are who are newly introduced, and newly worshipped [as we, by way of digression, have said already, and yet have left their places of worship desolate]; and for their temples, some of them are already left desolate, and others are built anew, according to the pleasure of men; whereas

they ought to have their opinion about God, and that worship which is due to him, always and immutably the same.

37. But now, this Apollonius Molo was one of these foolish and proud men. However, nothing that I have said was unknown to those that were real philosophers among the Greeks, nor were they unacquainted with those frigid pretensions of allegories [which had been alleged for such things]; on which account they justly despised them, but have still agreed with us as to the true and becoming notions of God; whence it was that Plato would not have political settlements admit to of any one of the other poets, and dismisses even Homer himself, with a garland on his head, and with ointment poured upon him, and this because he should not destroy the right notions of God with his fables. Nay, Plato principally imitated our legislator in this point, that he enjoined his citizens to have he main regard to this precept, "That every one of them should learn their laws accurately." He also ordained, that they should not admit of foreigners intermixing with their own people at random; and provided that the commonwealth should keep itself pure, and consist of such only as persevered in their own laws. Apollonius Molo did no way consider this, when he made it one branch of his accusation against us, that we do not admit of such as have different notions about God, nor will we have fellowship with those that choose to observe a way of living different from ourselves, yet is not this method peculiar to us, but common to all other men; not among the ordinary Grecians only, but among such of those Grecians as are of the greatest reputation among them. Moreover, the Lacedemonians continued in their way of expelling foreigners, and would not indeed give leave to their own people to travel abroad, as suspecting that those two things would introduce a dissolution of their own laws: and perhaps there may be some reason to blame the rigid severity of the Lacedemonians, for they bestowed the privilege of their city on no foreigners, nor indeed would give leave to them to stay among them; whereas we, though we do not think fit to imitate other institutions, yet do we willingly admit of those that desire to partake of ours, which, I think, I may reckon to be a plain indication of our humanity, and at the same time of our magnanimity also.

38. But I shall say no more of the Lacedemonians. As for the Athenians, who glory in having made their city to be common to all men, what their behavior was Apollonius did not know, while they punished those that did but speak one word contrary to the laws about the gods, without any mercy; for on what other account was it that Socrates was put to death by them? For certainly he neither betrayed their city to its enemies, nor was he guilty of any sacrilege with regard to any of their temples; but it was on this account, that he swore certain new oaths [26] and

that he affirmed either in earnest, or, as some say, only in jest, that a certain demon used to make signs to him [what he should not do]. For these reasons he was condemned to drink poison, and kill himself. His accuser also complained that he corrupted the young men, by inducing them to despise the political settlement and laws of their city: and thus was Socrates, the citizen of Athens, punished. There was also Anaxagoras, who, although he was of Clazomente, was within a few suffrages of being condemned to die, because he said the sun, which the Athenians thought to be a god, was a ball of fire. They also made this public proclamation, "That they would give a talent to any one who would kill Diagoras of Melos," because it was reported of him that he laughed at their mysteries. Protagoras also, who was thought to have written somewhat that was not owned for truth by the Athenians about the gods, had been seized upon, and put to death, if he had not fled away immediately. Nor need we at all wonder that they thus treated such considerable men, when they did not spare even women also; for they very lately slew a certain priestess, because she was accused by somebody that she initiated people into the worship of strange gods, it having been forbidden so to do by one of their laws; and a capital punishment had been decreed to such as introduced a strange god; it being manifest, that they who make use of such a law do not believe those of other nations to be really gods, otherwise they had not envied themselves the advantage of more gods than they already had. And this was the happy administration of the affairs of the Athenians! Now as to the Scythians, they take a pleasure in killing men, and differ but little from brute beasts; yet do they think it reasonable to have their institutions observed. They also slew Anacharsis, a person greatly admired for his wisdom among the Greeks, when he returned to them, because he appeared to come fraught with Grecian customs. One may also find many to have been punished among the Persians, on the very same account. And to be sure Apollonius was greatly pleased with the laws of the Persians, and was an admirer of them, because the Greeks enjoyed the advantage of their courage, and had the very same opinion about the gods which they had. This last was exemplified in the temples which they burnt, and their courage in coming, and almost entirely enslaving the Grecians. However, Apollonius has imitated all the Persian institutions, and that by his offering violence to other men's wives, and gelding his own sons. Now, with us, it is a capital crime, if any one does thus abuse even a brute beast; and as for us, neither hath the fear of our governors, nor a desire of following what other nations have in so great esteem, been able to withdraw us from our own laws; nor have we exerted our courage in raising up wars to increase our wealth, but only for the observation of our laws; and when we with patience bear other losses, yet when any persons would compel us to break our laws, then it is that we choose to go to war, though it be beyond our ability to pursue it, and bear the greatest calamities to the last with much fortitude. And, indeed, what reason can there be why we should desire to imitate the laws of other nations, while we see they are not observed by their own legislators [27] And why do not the Lacedemonians think of abolishing that form of their government which suffers them not to associate with any others, as well as their contempt of matrimony? And why do not the Eleans and Thebans abolish that unnatural and impudent lust, which makes them lie with males? For they will not show a sufficient sign of their repentance of what they of old thought to be very excellent, and very advantageous in their practices, unless they entirely avoid all such actions for the time to come: nay, such things are inserted into the body of their laws, and had once such a power among the Greeks, that they ascribed these sodomitical practices to the gods themselves, as a part of their good character; and indeed it was according to the same manner that the gods married their own sisters. This the Greeks contrived as an apology for their own absurd and unnatural pleasures.

39. I omit to speak concerning punishments, and how many ways of escaping them the greatest part of the legislators have afforded malefactors, by ordaining that, for adulteries, fines in money should be allowed, and for corrupting [28] [virgins] they need only marry them as also what excuses they may have in denying the facts, if any one attempts to inquire into them; for amongst most other nations it is a studied art how men may transgress their laws; but no such thing is permitted amongst us; for though we be deprived of our wealth, of our cities, or of the other advantages we have, our law continues immortal; nor can any Jew go so far from his own country, nor be so aftrighted at the severest lord, as not to be more aftrighted at the law than at him. If, therefore, this be the disposition we are under, with regard to the excellency of our laws, let our enemies make us this concession, that our laws are most excellent; and if still they imagine, that though we so firmly adhere to them, yet are they bad laws notwithstanding, what penalties then do they deserve to undergo who do not observe their own laws, which they esteem so far superior to them? Whereas, therefore, length of time is esteemed to be the truest touchstone in all cases, I would make that a testimonial of the excellency of our laws, and of that belief thereby delivered to us concerning God. For as there hath been a very long time for this comparison, if any one will but compare its duration with the duration of the laws made by other legislators, he will find our legislator to have been the ancientest of them all.

40. We have already demonstrated that our laws have been such as have always inspired admiration and imitation into all other men; nay, the earliest

Grecian philosophers, though in appearance they observed the laws of their own countries, yet did they, in their actions, and their philosophic doctrines, follow our legislator, and instructed men to live sparingly, and to have friendly communication one with another. Nay, further, the multitude of mankind itself have had a great inclination of a long time to follow our religious observances; for there is not any city of the Grecians, nor any of the barbarians, nor any nation whatsoever, whither our custom of resting on the seventh day hath not come, and by which our fasts and lighting up lamps, and many of our prohibitions as to our food, are not observed; they also endeavor to imitate our mutual concord with one another, and the charitable distribution of our goods, and our diligence in our trades, and our fortitude in undergoing the distresses we are in, on account of our laws; and, what is here matter of the greatest admiration, our law hath no bait of pleasure to allure men to it, but it prevails by its own force; and as God himself pervades all the world, so hath our law passed through all the world also. So that if any one will but reflect on his own country, and his own family, he will have reason to give credit to what I say. It is therefore but just, either to condemn all mankind of indulging a wicked disposition, when they have been so desirous of imitating laws that are to them foreign and evil in themselves, rather than following laws of their own that are of a better character, or else our accusers must leave off their spite against us. Nor are we guilty of any envious behavior towards them, when we honor our own legislator, and believe what he, by his prophetic authority, hath taught us concerning God. For though we should not be able ourselves to understand the excellency of our own laws, yet would the great multitude of those that desire to imitate them, justify us, in greatly valuing ourselves upon them.

41. But as for the [distinct] political laws by which we are governed, I have delivered them accurately in my books of Antiquities; and have only mentioned them now, so far as was necessary to my present purpose, without proposing to myself either to blame the laws of other nations, or to make an encomium upon our own; but in order to convict those that have written about us unjustly, and in an impudent affectation of disguising the truth. And now I think I have sufficiently completed what I proposed in writing these books. For whereas our accusers have pretended that our nation are a people of very late original, I have demonstrated that they are exceeding ancient; for I have produced as witnesses thereto many ancient writers, who have made mention of us in their books, while they had said that no such writer had so done. Moreover, they had said that we were sprung from the Egyptians, while I have proved that we came from another country into Egypt: while they had told lies of us, as if we were expelled thence on

account of diseases on our bodies, it has appeared, on the contrary, that we returned to our country by our own choice, and with sound and strong bodies. Those accusers reproached our legislator as a vile fellow; whereas God in old time bare witness to his virtuous conduct; and since that testimony of God, time itself hath been discovered to have borne witness to the same thing.

42. As to the laws themselves, more words are unnecessary, for they are visible in their own nature, and appear to teach not impiety, but the truest piety in the world. They do not make men hate one another, but encourage people to communicate what they have to one another freely; they are enemies to injustice, they take care of righteousness, they banish idleness and expensive living, and instruct men to be content with what they have, and to be laborious in their calling; they forbid men to make war from a desire of getting more, but make men courageous in defending the laws; they are inexorable in punishing malefactors; they admit no sophistry of words, but are always established by actions themselves, which actions we ever propose as surer demonstrations than what is contained in writing only: on which account I am so bold as to say that we are become the teachers of other men, in the greatest number of things, and those of the most excellent nature only; for what is more excellent than inviolable piety? what is more just than submission to laws? and what is more advantageous than mutual love and concord? and this so far that we are to be neither divided by calamities, nor to become injurious and seditious in prosperity; but to contemn death when we are in war, and in peace to apply ourselves to our mechanical occupations, or to our tillage of the ground; while we in all things and all ways are satisfied that God is the inspector and governor of our actions. If these precepts had either been written at first, or more exactly kept by any others before us, we should have owed them thanks as disciples owe to their masters; but if it be visible that we have made use of them more than any other men, and if we have demonstrated that the original invention of them is our own, let the Apions, and the Molons, with all the rest of those that delight in lies and reproaches, stand confuted; but let this and the foregoing book be dedicated to thee, Epaphroditus, who art so great a lover of truth, and by thy means to those that have been in like manner desirous to be acquainted with the affairs of our nation.

APION BOOK II: FOOTNOTES

[1] The former part of this second book is written against the calumnies of Apion, and then, more briefly, against the like calumnies of Apollonius Molo. But after that, Josephus leaves off any more particular reply to those adversaries of the Jews, and gives us a large and excellent description and vindication of that

theocracy which was settled for the Jewish nation by Moses, their great legislator.

[2] Called by Tiberius Cymbalum Mundi, The drum of the world.

[3] This seems to have been the first dial that had been made in Egypt, and was a little before the time that Ahaz made his [first] dial in Judea, and about anno 755, in the first year of the seventh olympiad, as we shall see presently. See 2 Kings 20:11; Isaiah 38:8.

[4] The burial-place for dead bodies, as I suppose.

[5] Here begins a great defect in the Greek copy; but the old Latin version fully supplies that defect.

[6] What error is here generally believed to have been committed by our Josephus in ascribing a deliverance of the Jews to the reign of Ptolemy Physco, the seventh of those Ptolemus, which has been universally supposed to have happened under Ptolemy Philopater, the fourth of them, is no better than a gross error of the moderns, and not of Josephus, as I have fully proved in the Authentic. Rec. Part I. p. 200-201, whither I refer the inquisitive reader.

[7] Sister's son, and adopted son.

[8] Called more properly Molo, or Apollonius Molo, as hereafter; for Apollonins, the son of Molo, was another person, as Strabo informs us, lib. xiv.

[9] Furones in the Latin, which what animal it denotes does not now appear.

[10] It is great pity that these six pagan authors, here mentioned to have described the famous profanation of the Jewish temple by Antiochus Epiphanes, should be all lost; I mean so far of their writings as contained that description; though it is plain Josephus perused them all as extant in his time.

[11] It is remarkable that Josephus here, and, I think, no where else, reckons up four distinct courts of the temple; that of the Gentiles, that of the women of Israel, that of the men of Israel, and that of the priests; as also that the court of the women admitted of the men, [I suppose only of the husbands of those wives that were therein,] while the court of the men did not admit any women into it at all.

[12] Judea, in the Greek, by a gross mistake of the transcribers.

[13] Seven in the Greek, by a like gross mistake of the transcribers. See of the War, B. V. ch. 5. sect. 4.

[14] Two hundred in the Greek, contrary to the twenty in the War, B. VII. ch, 5. sect. 3.

[15] This notorious disgrace belonging peculiarly to the people of Egypt, ever since the times of the old prophets of the Jews, noted both sect. 4 already, and here, may be confirmed by the testimony of Isidorus, an Egyptian of Pelusium, Epist. lib. i. Ep. 489. And this is a remarkable completion of the ancient prediction of God by Ezekiel 29:14, 15, "that the Egyptians should be a base

kingdom, the basest of the kingdoms," and that, "it should not exalt itself any more above the nations."

[16] The truth of which still further appears by the present observation of Josephus, that these Egyptians had never, in all the past ages since Sesostris, had one day of liberty, no, not so much as to have been free from despotic power under any of the monarchies to that day. And all this has been found equally true in the latter ages, under the Romans, Saracens, Mamelukes, and Turks, from the days of Josephus till the present ago also.

[17] This language, that Moses, "persuaded himself" that what he did was according to God's will, can mean no more, by Josephus's own constant notions elsewhere, than that he was "firmly persuaded," that he had "fully satisfied himself" that so it was, viz. by the many revelations he had received from God, and the numerous miracles God had enabled him to work, as he both in these very two books against Apion, and in his Antiquities, most clearly and frequently assures us. This is further evident from several passages lower, where he affirms that Moses was no impostor nor deceiver, and where he assures that Moses's constitution of government was no other than a theocracy; and where he says they are to hope for deliverance out of their distresses by prayer to God, and that withal it was owing in part to this prophetic spirit of Moses that the Jews expected a resurrection from the dead. See almost as strange a use of the like words, "to persuade God," Antiq. B. VI. ch. 5. sect. 6.

[18] That is, Moses really was, what the heathen legislators pretended to be, under a Divine direction; nor does it yet appear that these pretensions to a supernatural conduct, either in these legislators or oracles, were mere delusions of men without any demoniacal impressions, nor that Josephus took them so to be; as the ancientest and contemporary authors did still believe them to be supernatural.

[19] This whole very large passage is corrected by Dr. Hudson from Eusebius's citation of it, Prep. Evangel. viii. 8, which is here not a little different from the present MSS. of Josephus.

[20] This expression itself, that "Moses ordained the Jewish government to be a theocracy," may be illustrated by that parallel expression in the Antiquities, B. III. ch. 8. sect. 9, that "Moses left it to God to be present at his sacrifices when he pleased; and when he pleased, to be absent." Both ways of speaking sound harsh in the ears of Jews and Christians, as do several others which Josephus uses to the heathens; but still they were not very improper in him, when he all along thought fit to accommodate himself, both in his Antiquities, and in these his books against Apion, all written for the use of the Greeks and Romans, to their notions and

language, and this as far as ever truth would give him leave. Though it be very observable withal, that he never uses such expressions in his books of the War, written originally for the Jews beyond Euphrates, and in their language, in all these cases. However, Josephus directly supposes the Jewish settlement, under Moses, to be a Divine settlement, and indeed no other than a real theocracy.

[21] These excellent accounts of the Divine attributes, and that God is not to be at all known in his essence, as also some other clear expressions about the resurrection of the dead, and the state of departed souls, etc., in this late work of Josephus, look more like the exalted notions of the Essens, or rather Ebionite Christians, than those of a mere Jew or Pharisee. The following large accounts also of the laws of Moses, seem to me to show a regard to the higher interpretations and improvements of Moses's laws, derived from Jesus Christ, than to the bare letter of them in the Old Testament, whence alone Josephus took them when he wrote his Antiquities; nor, as I think, can some of these laws, though generally excellent in their kind, be properly now found either in the copies of the Jewish Pentateuch, or in Philo, or in Josephus himself, before he became a Nazarene or Ebionite Christian; nor even all of them among the laws of catholic Christianity themselves. I desire, therefore, the learned reader to consider, whether some of these improvements or interpretations might not be peculiar to the Essens among the Jews, or rather to the Nazarenes or Ebionites among the Christians, though we have indeed but imperfect accounts of those Nazarenes or Ebionite Christians transmitted down to us at this day.

[22] We may here observe how known a thing it was among the Jews and heathens, in this and many other instances, that sacrifices were still accompanied with prayers; whence most probably came those phrases of "the sacrifice of prayer, the sacrifice of praise, the sacrifice of thanksgiving." However, those ancient forms used at sacrifices are now generally lost, to the no small damage of true religion. It is here also exceeding remarkable, that although the temple at Jerusalem was built as the only place where the whole nation of the Jews were to offer their sacrifices, yet is there no mention of the "sacrifices" themselves, but of "prayers" only, in Solomon's long and famous form of devotion at its dedication, 1 Kings 8.; 2 Chronicles 6. See also many passages cited in the Apostolical Constitutions, VII. 37, and Of the War, above, B. VII. ch. 5. sect. 6.

[23] This text is no where in our present copies of the Old Testament.

[24] It may not be amiss to set down here a very remarkable testimony of the great philosopher Cicero, as to the preference of "laws to philosophy:—I will," says he, "boldly declare my opinion, though the whole world be offended at it. I prefer this little book of the Twelve Tables alone to all the volumes of the philosophers.

I find it to be not only of more weight,' but also much more useful."—Oratore.

[25] We have observed our times of rest, and sorts of food allowed us [Footnote during our distresses].

[26] See what those novel oaths were in Dr. Hudson's note, viz. to swear by an oak, by a goat, and by a dog, as also by a gander, as say Philostratus and others. This swearing strange oaths was also forbidden by the Tyrians, B. I. sect. 22, as Spanheim here notes.

[27] Why Josephus here should blame some heathen legislators, when they allowed so easy a composition for simple fornication, as an obligation to marry the virgin that was corrupted, is hard to say, seeing he had himself truly informed us that it was a law of the Jews, Antiq. B. IV. ch. 8. sect. 23, as it is the law of Christianity also: see Horeb Covenant, p. 61. I am almost ready to suspect that, for, we should here read, and that corrupting wedlock, or other men's wives, is the crime for which these heathens wickedly allowed this composition in money.

[28] Or "for corrupting other men's wives the same allowance."

www.ingramcontent.com/pod-product-compliance
Lightning Source LLC
Chambersburg PA
CBHW031416040426
42444CB00005B/596